THE HIGH IMPACT LEADER

Moments Matter in Accelerating Authentic Leadership Development

Bruce J. Avolio
Fred Luthans

New York   Chicago   San Francisco   Lisbon
London   Madrid   Mexico City   Milan   New Delhi
San Juan   Seoul   Singapore   Sydney   Toronto

1 2 3 4 5 6 7 8 9 0   DOC/DOC   0 9 8 7 6 5

ISBN 0–07–144413–0

McGraw-Hill books are available at special quantity discounts to use as premiums and sales promotions, or for use in corporate training programs. For more information, please write to the Director of Special Sales, Professional Publishing, McGraw-Hill, Two Penn Plaza, New York, NY 10121–2298. Or contact your local bookstore.

 This book is printed on recycled, acid-free paper containing a minimum of 50% recycled de-inked fiber.

Library of Congress Cataloging-in-Publication Data

Avolio, Bruce J.
     The high impact leader : moments matter in accelerating authentic leadership / by Bruce J. Avolio and Fred Luthans.
         p.   cm.
     ISBN 0-07-144413-0 (hardcover : alk. paper) 1. Leadership.
I. Luthans, Fred. II. Title.
HM1261.A948 2005
158'.4—dc22

                                        2005010066

To our wives, children, other family members,
friends, teachers, colleagues, and students
that have provided us with the very best
"Moments That Mattered" to our life developement.

Thank you.

CONTENTS

PREFACE:
AUTHENTIC LEADERSHIP
DEVELOPMENT

ONE OF THE MAIN REASONS that we wrote this book was to shift the attention on leadership development from what typically occurs in planned interventions to all possible moments that could positively impact upon your leadership development. These "moments that matter" can be planned or unplanned, but our intent for the book is to facilitate and accelerate your authentic leadership development, or what we simply refer to as ALD.

Another reason we wrote *The High Impact Leader* is that there are a lot of leadership development efforts out there that in our view fall short of being genuine or authentic. Indeed, we are dismayed at how few leadership development programs actually can substantiate that even one leader has been developed as a consequence of most of these programs. This is surprising, given the billions invested each year on the premise that attending a leadership development program will actually enhance one's leadership potential and capability.

As we discuss in this book, life's program is perhaps the most authentic contributor to advancing one's leadership development. Our goal is to try and accelerate your life's program, by augmenting it with authentic leadership development practices. However, it's important to note that we are not trying to replace life's program as a main source for driving your leadership development—nor could we. Indeed, we have tried to convey, in every chapter, how to work with life's program to advance your authentic leadership development. We put particular emphasis on extracting from both negative and positive moments in order to determine how you view yourself.

ACCELERATING ALD

We have attempted to create a practical framework to accelerate your authentic leadership development, or what we call ALD. We provide a methodology, a broad range of exercises, and a rationale for engaging you in increasing your self-awareness and accelerating your authentic leadership potential.

We have specifically focused on moments that matter in one's life, which often seem inconsequential but can profoundly shape one's destiny in terms of effective leadership practices. We propose you take the time to understand the nature of such moments and how they impact your personal model of leadership.

We encourage you throughout the book to consider that each and every moment can matter to your ALD. In addition to your own ALD, such moments can also accelerate the development of others, if reflected upon and incorporated into how you go about influencing them to achieve their full potential.

OVERVIEW OF THE BOOK

We begin in the introduction and first chapter by discussing how leaders have to bring the "future to the present," especially with respect to their own ALD. We use popular concepts in the field of cognitive psychology, concepts arguing that everyone has a working model of the self. This is labeled their "actual self." To move to the future, one must consider the "possible self," or what one can become.

Generally, moments in life trigger what is possible. In the ALD process, leaders move from what they view as being possible in their development to what they actually do. In other words, in ALD, the possible becomes the actual; that is, the future becomes the present.

Another main point we highlight early in the book is that we focus too much attention and energy on negative moments. We tend to lose the potential to develop that comes from often overlooked positive moments. Not to get overly academic, but we would argue that everyone has an implicit theory of what they believe constitutes their leadership. In order to develop that theory, one must be willing to analyze and challenge it. Positive moments often trigger those challenges and result in ALD. We also know that negative moments do the same.

In the second chapter, we provide the results of a national poll that we conducted on authentic leadership. Our intent in conducting this poll was to provide a basis for you to compare your leadership, as well as the leadership of others around you, to a national benchmark. We also provide a Web site, www.e=leading.com that you can go to with your pin number, found on the cover jacket flap after our bids, to take the survey yourself.

In the third chapter we summarize the last 100 years of research on leadership interventions and development. Our goal in presenting this research is to provide a solid foundation upon which you and others can genuinely develop authentic leadership. By looking back over the last 100 years, we are able to show that leadership interventions can work.

Perhaps the most important implication from this massive study is getting people to believe that leadership interventions do indeed work. We end the chapter by demonstrating that leadership is both made and born. Although genetics seems to account for about a third of the emergence of leaders, trigger moments are also a force in determining how leaders actually develop.

In Chapter 4 we introduce a map for ALD to help guide you toward achieving your own successful leadership intervention. We place a lot of emphasis on what actually comprises self-awareness and how one translates this self-awareness into authentic leadership development. Self-awareness is not bipolar. Rather, it is on a continuum that can be reinforced by self-reflection and by thus taking advantage of trigger moments that are both planned and unplanned.

Chapter 5 focuses more specifically on the link between one's actual self and possible self and how movement occurs from one to the other. We discuss how relevant others in your life can facilitate the movement from the actual to the possible. This is especially true if you remain aware of their roles in this process. You are also part of that developmental process for others who are trying to accomplish the same thing: develop their authentic leadership potential. The chapter emphasizes the discipline of staying focused on understanding one's actual self in order to move to what is possible. To a large degree, to know more about ourselves, we must learn to slow down how fast we process information about ourselves.

In Chapter 6 we emphasize the importance of writing the story of your leadership life that you want to create. We all narrate life in our own unique ways, and leadership is no different. Thus, once we know the future we want to bring to the present, we have to create the scripts in our mind to move to that future point.

In this chapter we point out how often we let others author the life course we are going to pursue. Too often, in fact, we simply leave it up to whatever is going to happen. ALD means determining how you want your leadership life's story to unfold. The ALD process helps you take advantage of the special moments as they arise. The planned or unplanned moments can accelerate you toward the goals you have set for your authentic leadership.

So, in this chapter we talk about the depths to learning about one's self. We also provide the framework and stimulation to help structure the future direction you intend to pursue, and to regulate how you'll bring the future to the present. Self-regulation provides the discipline and compass in executing your leadership development reliably and ethically.

Chapter 7 introduces you to what we call psychological capital, or simply PsyCap. Using both human and social capital as a point of departure, we specifically identify what we mean by PsyCap, and in our discussion focus on positive strengths such as confidence, hope, optimism, and resiliency. We review how each of these capacities contribute to having a positive orientation toward leading others, and how authentic leaders build PsyCap in followers. We propose that this PsyCap be monitored as a means of determining the extent to which organizational leaders and their followers are achieving their full potential. Investing in both leaders' and followers' PsyCap can return competitive advantage to today's organizations.

Chapter 8 builds on Chapter 7, discussing how leaders and followers go about enhancing the value of their PsyCap. We make the connection that as one's leadership becomes more genuine and authentic, the desired self and the actual self become one in the same, resulting in a more positive outlook and performance impact. The strong correspondence between how I thought I viewed myself and how I actually am as a leader results in greater positive PsyCap.

Again, we discuss the importance of positive beliefs in energizing both leaders and followers to achieve their maximum potential growth and sustainable, veritable performance. In this chapter we also provide specific opportunities for you to measure your own level of PsyCap and to evaluate your social network by going to our Web site at the University of Nebraska, Gallup Leadership Institute, which was set up for this purpose.

In Chapter 9 we discuss what constitutes sustainable and veritable performance. To determine whether leadership development has occurred, a performance impact point must be identified and monitored. Here we focus on the changing nature of what constitutes effective performance. Unfortunately, in today's hypercompetitive environment, it has become necessary for leaders and followers to continually grow to simply keep up with what is considered "typical performance."

In other words, as the standards for performance are increasingly raised in all performance domains, it is essential for leaders, their associates, and the organization to grow in order to simply achieve each new minimum standard of performance accomplishment. We discuss the levels of performance that one can monitor and also the elements that comprise those levels. Our main purpose in this stage of the ALD process is to direct development to where it really matters—at the point of performance impact.

Depending upon the leader to be monitored, this performance may be typical or extraordinary. We also give attention to how the leadership indirectly affects sustainable, veritable performance, and how the culture and climate of the organization contributes to such performance. Although we give numerous examples of effective and ineffective dimensions of authentic leaders throughout the book, we end the chapter by presenting someone we are willing to go on record as saying meets the criteria for what we feel constitutes an authentic leader: Warren Buffett.

Finally, in Chapter 10 we move from our detailed presentation of the ALD process to providing a specific structure for you to do your own ALD plan. In all nine previous chapters, we try to involve you as much as possible, but in this last chapter we ask you to take what you have learned and focus it directly on your own authentic leadership development.

In the final chapter we describe a number of individuals who went through trigger moments and determined how they would use them to accelerate their development as leaders. To engineer your trigger moments, we provide 10 simple rules and a dozen guidelines for effective authentic leadership. They should to stimulate your thinking about ALD. Then, we provide you with an open-ended plan for ALD for you to complete. In other words, we end this book with your input, not ours, which is the essence of what authentic leadership development should be all about.

LEADERSHIP NOTES

- Many leadership development programs fall short in their content and delivery.
- Both positive and negative moments can help to accelerate authentic leadership development (ALD).
- Positive beliefs, or PsyCap, can strengthen both leaders and followers and help make the entire organization more effective.

INTRODUCTION: BRINGING YOUR FUTURE TO THE PRESENT

"In matters of style, swim with the current; in matters of principle, stand like a rock."

—*Thomas Jefferson*

YOU MIGHT ASK: Why another book on leadership? We can all agree that leadership at all levels of society and organizations is more important than ever, but can it really be taught in classrooms or learned from a book?

We both come from academic backgrounds. For a combined total of 65 years, we have studied, theorized, researched, trained, consulted, coached, and written about leadership. As important, we have also practiced leadership in our various professional roles (and some real jobs) through the years. At this stage of our own development in the leadership field, we are passionately convinced that there are tried-and-true ways to help accelerate your authentic leadership development.

Before we go any further, we want to differentiate and precisely define what we mean by authentic leadership development, or ALD. In our academic theory-building papers, we draw from both one's life course and positive psychological capital—i.e., psychological states such as confidence, hope, optimism, and resiliency, which are open to development, as opposed to fixed traits—as well as strength-based cultures/contexts that support authentic leadership development. As additional and significant input, we also include one's ethical and moral perspective, when all of this combined leads to greater self-awareness and positive performance impact on leaders, followers, and organizations. Thus, we formally define ALD as:

> The process that draws upon a leader's life course, psychological capital, moral perspective, and a "highly developed" supporting organizational climate to produce greater self-awareness and self-regulated positive behaviors, which in turn foster continuous, positive self-development resulting in veritable, sustained performance.

We felt it was important that you get this "long-winded" definition right away. Our intent is to not only assert that, unlike many previous books on leadership written for real-world managers, this book is truly based on our considerable theory and basic research background, but also to let you know it is not a simple process.

However, as a working and perhaps more friendly definition for the rest of the book, it is important to remember that, like retired Medtronic CEO Bill George's recent best-selling book, *Authentic Leadership,* ALD emphasizes authenticity of being true and aware of one's self and to others. But ALD is also different from his book and others by focusing on the *developmental process* that achieves that end goal.

Our proposed ALD does not dismiss the now recognized importance that heredity, life's events, and actually experiencing leadership plays in its development. We tend to agree with Henry Mintzberg's recent observation that "leadership and management are part of life, and education cannot teach life experience to those who haven't acquired it. You cannot learn to lead an organization from a classroom." We simply assert that what we now know about the authentic leadership development process, as presented in this book, can develop you faster than life's unfolding program, with less risk, and possibly with greater positive impact.

Specifically, we will demonstrate how to level the playing field for those not born with or fortunate enough to experience life's situations that "naturally" accelerate ALD. Our purpose is to shift attention from the focus over the last 100 years on what a leadership development program should include, to focusing on the newly emerging ALD process.

Make no mistake: We do not shy away from suggesting best leadership development practices and providing plenty of normative examples. However, this book is concerned with the processes situated or "embedded" in the life span of individuals in order to accelerate the positive development of authentic leadership. In particular, we challenge the notion that significant ALD only occurs after adapting to painful life events such as being unjustly fired, losing a loved one, or suffering a heart attack. These negative events are only a part of the larger ALD process. We will demonstrate throughout that there are also positive moments that matter in ALD.

MOMENTS ARE THE KEY

Let's shift gears a moment and make a hypothetical call around the globe for a moratorium on leadership development programs. Let's say at the beginning of next month all leadership development programs must cease to operate. Now, fast-forward five years and do a global poll on the leadership effectiveness of organizations. Do you believe we would have a dramatically worse picture of leadership than if we continued to spend accelerating billions a year on leadership development interventions?

Under the current state of leadership development, our speculation is that people would develop, through the natural course of events, or by proactively finding ways to use positive experiences. Either with or without more existing leadership development programs, we feel the world and its organizations would frankly be no better or worse. Indeed, an interesting proposal might be to eliminate all existing leadership development efforts and instead support life's leadership development program, rather than the other way around.

Our intent is to make leadership development more real and genuine, and to focus on the moments that matter. We are trying to get it as close—but not too close—to what leaders actually have to do in order to develop and achieve positive, sustainable results. We want to do this without sacrificing learning and development. Although we hope your reading experience will be real and have a direct impact on you, we also want it to be realistic, not prescriptive. ALD is still a personal, true-self, process.

Of course, the hypothetical suggestion about suspending all leadership development efforts would never happen. There is way too much invested in the status quo and to the tendency to latch onto the latest buzz words and silver bullets. Yet there is little or no evidence that this investment is paying off. For example, the featured companies in the well-known book *In Search of Excellence,* one of the best-selling business books in history, fell on hard times soon after the book was published.

One analysis found that $100 invested in Peters and Waterman's "excellent" firms yielded a median return of $613, while tossing a dart blindfolded at any fund based on the S&P 500 produced a 22 percent higher $752. The same is true of almost all existing leadership development programs. There's not an ounce of proof that they have developed even one authentic leader.

Remember that we are talking about *authentic* leadership, and not functional leadership knowledge and techniques. We would seriously ask how many of today's leadership programs have actually developed one authentic leader . . . faster and better than life's program? Moreover, ask yourself the pragmatic question: How many organizations do you know that still invest in leadership development programs while at the same time significantly cutting their operating budget? If these companies honestly believed that their programs had produced the leaders needed to move the organization ahead— and had proof to that effect—don't you think they would do everything they could to keep them funded? But support for such programs is not what we've been hearing over the years. Instead, leadership consultants commiserate and complain that in our uncertain economy "right-sizing" companies in trouble are pulling out resources from leadership development programs.

So again we ask: What evidence has been provided to show that just one leader has been developed better than life's program has accomplished? Honestly, after years of study, we simply don't know of many "industrial strength" programs that have produced such evidence. The reason is, most leadership development programs violate the basic rule of what constitutes effective leadership itself, which is to know your end goal before you start.

Indeed, most leadership development programs have no clear end, or terminal learning or performance impact goal. The unfortunate truth is that virtually all these programs have no idea what achieving successful leadership development actually looks like. Of course, if we knew what it looked like, and there was actually some metrics to determine whether it was achieved, we would be a lot further along in accelerating leadership development faster than what life can do on its own.

This leads to our simple goal for *The High Impact Leader*. We want to identify what the authentic leadership process truly looks like. We submit it is better to support life's program, and make it the focal point of a leadership program, than to pour more money and effort into today's mainline leadership development programs, with no understanding of the process or what the goals are. We submit that over the last 100 years this has been the case; we would have been as well off with life's program.

We will begin, in the first chapter, by describing the authentic leadership development process (we will tend to use ALD from here on) and what we mean when we say it is authentic. To do so, we must consider that ALD involves situations, events, and experiences in life that have an impact on how leaders view who they are, what they want to achieve, and how they choose to go about influencing others to achieve their end goal, and hopefully to influence their followers as well.

Moshe Rubenstein, a distinguished faculty member from UCLA, started his discussion with a group of "co-learners" in our new, innovative, University of Nebraska/Gallup MBA/MA program in authentic leadership development declaring: "Leaders bring the future to the present."

This statement is something we all can marvel over. We wonder how it is possible. Conventional wisdom prescribes that leaders must have that "vision thing," but how does one picture the future, grab it, and then bring it into the present for inquiry? How did Mandela do this for South Africa, in his worst moments on Robben's Island? How did Harriet Tubman do this, in her most dangerous moments transferring black slaves from the South to the North through the underground railroad?

How did Oprah Winfrey, born and raised in a single-parent family in racially prejudiced Kosciusko, Mississippi, become the most successful businesswoman in the world? How did Bill Wilson do so, sitting in a café in Akron, Ohio, discussing his vision for Alcoholics Anonymous? How about Roberto C. Goizueta, who built Coke into a global force? Or Ricardo Semler, who took his Brazilian firm Semco from $34 million to $212 million over the last 10 years through an unorthodox style, which inluded new hires wandering through the company for a year to see what they wanted to do? How did each of these leaders bring the future into their present, and then change the present to be receptive to the future envisioned?

Like any leader, you, as well as we, as authors, are placed here at the same point of departure while together embarking on our journey of authentic leadership development. Many books have eloquently (and not so eloquently) presented how leaders should be developed. However, very few, if any, have actually brought the future into the present in terms of what the process looks like, and then engaged readers to enhance their own ALD.

In our view, it is easier to envision the person (you, the reader, in this case) in the future than in the extremely complex process that created that person. In fact, we feel this is a major reason why we have not yet brought the leadership development process from the future to the present. We intend to bring your future as an authentic leader to your reading of this book, hopefully with developmental consequences.

YOUR FIRST ALD EXERCISE

To truly make this journey a developmental experience, we strongly urge you, at minimum, to think through and reflect on each of the questions or requests at the end of each chapter, which we will initiate here. Preferably, we would like you to keep a journal with notes and ideas as you read the chapters, and write out answers to these chapter-ending exercises. This is one way to take ownership in your authentic leadership development.

1. Wherever you are in your life course, think back to various specific moments that accelerated your ability to effectively

influence others to work toward a particularly challenging goal.

2. Now, isolate one important leadership moment that stands out in your life, and then think about the situation or context in which that moment arose.

3. What was your emotion (heart-felt feelings) in that moment, and what is it right now?

4. What were you trying to do?

5. What were others trying to do?

6. What did you achieve, and what did others achieve?

7. If you could go back and change any aspect of that moment, or surrounding that moment, what would you alter? Why?

8. What did you learn?

9. What have you taught others from this lesson?

10. Now create an important leadership moment in your future and bring it back to where you are right now. How can that moment be used to develop yourself and others?

11. Is there another moment you want to bring from the future to the present to have the same effect? (Now, you are bringing the future to the present.)

At this point, jot down what you have learned in your journal. Remember, if you're just reading (without keeping a journal), you are probably not developing to the fullest potential, and you have not taken all the steps to optimize your development process. There is no pressure to do this (we will not grade you!), but have fun with it, and the dividends in this small investment should pay off.

LEADERSHIP NOTES

- *The reality is, most leadership development programs fail.* This is because few programs out there have clear or terminal

learning or performance metrics; the managers who implement them are in the dark when it comes to successful leadership.
- *The most effective leaders "bring the future to the present."* This entails envisioning the future and making the present "receptive" to the future the leader envisions.

Make sure to keep a journal so you can respond to the exercises and questions that appear throughout the book. This will ensure that you are making the most of the research and advice in the book.

1

MOMENTS MATTER

THE CEO OF A SENIOR management group in a large telecom-munications company opened a recent meeting by saying he wanted to relay some personal issues he had been through over the past year, issues that had profoundly impacted his leadership. He then went on to describe in detail how he had come to a meeting just like the one they were now holding and realized that he was not feeling well. He left the meeting, and the next morning he was on the operating table going through quadruple bypass heart surgery. He told the group that this particular life event had totally reshaped his thinking about who he wanted to be and what he wanted to accomplish; what cognitive psychologists call his "possible self."

This event, and what transpired afterward, can be viewed as a leadership development "jolt," a turning point, or what we will simply call a "moment." It changed how he viewed himself and his role as a leader.

Around the table, many of his managers were nodding in agree-ment and acknowledging that the moment he described had been significant in changing his views about himself and his leadership of others. They had clearly noticed the change. This was an emotional, reflective, positive event for this leader's team based on a threatening, negative moment in his life's course.

Although somewhat eerie—but in retrospect fairly typical in today's executive suites—the next manager who spoke up also talked about his heart attack. He related how he had come to a point of deep realization of what he wanted to accomplish as a leader, stating that for him the surgery was also a defining moment in his life and in his leadership. Each manager felt that it was turning these events into something positive that developed their greater potential as leaders. As we often do these days, you might ask how many leadership development programs count on clogged arteries to positively accelerate authentic development in leaders.

Bruce (we will refer to ourselves, the authors, as Bruce or Fred, when appropriate) was the third person to speak at the meeting, and he facetiously asked the group if they thought that leadership development required quadruple bypass surgery. The managers nervously chuckled and raised their eyebrows. Then Bruce went on to exclaim: "I sure would like to make leadership development easier than open heart surgery!"

THE ALD CONTINUUM

So is leadership development somewhere between heart surgery and the typical one- to three-day miracle program that takes one to "the peak"?

Put simply, yes. Authentic leadership development does not necessarily have to coincide with cataclysmic life events. Indeed, ALD may even be accelerated by something positive. Unfortunately, on the other end of the continuum ALD likely does not occur in just a one- or even five-day program. At best, the beginning of change may be rooted or stimulated in these widely used programs.

In this book, you will learn that ALD is essentially something that happens both across one's life span and in unexpected negative or positive moments. These critical ALD moments may occur in any setting or circumstance. Moments that matter for ALD may happen while growing up, at social gatherings, at work, in the gym, on a bike trail, or in a church, temple, or mosque.

For example, entertainment and business leader Oprah Winfrey told Sidney Poitier the moment for her occurred when she was 10 years old watching TV from the linoleum floor of her mother's walk-up flat. She saw Poitier receive an Academy Award, and said to herself at that moment, "If he can do that, I wonder what I could do?" Besides these life events, such positive moments may even occur in a leadership development classroom, training center, retreat, coaching session, or hopefully while reading this book.

Very simply, authentic leadership development occurs when the "theory of one's leadership"—what leadership academics call the "implicit theory" in one's head—is challenged. In this moment of challenge, or during a period of reflection—somewhere between heart surgery and an interesting suggestion or observation—you ask yourself how you can better move others to the goals you and they want to achieve.

We must positively challenge the theory, model, and script that guide your leadership style.

Recently named Nobel Prize–winning behavioral decision theorist Daniel Kahneman (and fellow senior scientist with us at Gallup) says that people have potentially thousands of such moments every day. For some, these moments have immediate impact, while for others it might take three months, a year, or even five years before they realize what it meant to their development as a leader.

The well-known leadership writer Warren Bennis, in retrospective reflection in a recent *Harvard Business Review* article, revealed his own moment, one that shaped his personal theory of leadership to this day. He recalled being a very green 19-year-old lieutenant in World War II reporting to the front lines in Belgium. He arrived in the middle of the night at a bombed-out building and was offered a relatively comfortable bench in the kitchen to sleep on. Instead, he chose to throw his bag down with the rest of the sleeping men.

When the men began to wake in the morning, he overheard one sergeant ask the other, "Who's that?"

"That's our new platoon leader," was the reply.

"Good," the first sergeant said. "We can use him."

We would say this was an important moment for Bennis's personal theory of leadership. He explained as follows. As he puts it:

> My entry had been low key. I hadn't come in with my new commission blazing . . . I learned that they needed me—or, at least, they needed the person they would subsequently teach me to be.

BUILDING YOUR THEORY OF ALD

Leadership theory in one's head shaped by life's moments is not an academic theory at all, but rather, what academic theories such as ours attempt to explain. It is your personal theory, model, or story of how you want to influence others. We like the word "story" to describe this personal leadership theory. Why? If you read many biographies of well-known leaders, they almost always tell the life "story" of their leadership development, never the wonderful leadership development program they attended.

Think of your leadership development theory as being a story to guide you.

For example, we frequently find male leaders talking about the profound influence their mothers had on their development. Former President Clinton, for instance, said he was the product of an adoring mom. And former G.E. head Jack Welch, in his autobiography, gives complete credit to his powerhouse of a mother, who constantly challenged him to face reality and do better. And then there's the well-known European business tycoon Richard Branson, whose mother set very high expectations for him by telling everyone he would someday become prime minister of England, and who convinced him he could do whatever he set his mind to do.

These biographical anecdotes are a way of bringing the past to the present in the form of a story. It is useful for us to use such stories to bring the future to the present as it pertains to the ALD process.

Bruce, in the first class of a leadership forum he presented, asked a group of 18-year-olds—as a class of emerging leaders—to describe a moment that had positively impacted their development. One student said that he'd been a Boy Scout growing up, but when he reached ninth grade, all of his friends had quit and were telling him that he should "grow up" too! He loved the Boy Scouts but was afraid to challenge his friends. He decided he would stay on with the Scouts, and did through high school. In the moment he was relating this story, he realized that it was the first time he had taken a stand for himself, and it felt good, for it made him realize he could determine his own course.

Fortunately, there are enough common themes across all our unique personal theories or stories to come up with a more general theory that we can learn from and develop. If you remember the formal definition of our theory of ALD (which we will expand upon in Chapter 4), a fundamental starting point for ALD is self-awareness.

Such self-knowledge continues to serve our growth and development throughout life. Some event or moment causes you to deepen your understanding of your self, who you are, what you fear, and what you believe is possible. As you get to what is possible, you begin to formulate the future in the present.

BRINGING THE FUTURE TO THE PRESENT

In the business periodical *Fast Company*, a great story of bringing the future to the present takes place when the staff of a huge GM assembly plant is told by a corporate "suit" perched at a podium that the plant is to be shut down. He declares, "There is nothing you can do to affect this decision."

It became a moment for the plant manager, who turned this negative ultimatum into a positive impact on his leadership. After the dust had settled and the corporate representative had left, he swallowed hard and addressed his shocked workers: "There may be nothing we can do to affect this decision, but there is something we can do: We can make them feel really stupid! Because they are going to be closing the best plant in General Motors!"

This impassioned speech got everyone behind him, and "Be the best!" became the rallying cry, with everyone working hard to accomplish a common goal. Within two years the factory was indeed the lowest-cost producer with the lowest warranty costs, and GM "ate crow" and kept the plant open. The plant manager had clearly made another interpretation of this moment brought on by the corporate ultimatum. He brought the future to the present, changed his personal theory of leadership, and attained incredibly positive performance results.

Bruce heard a firsthand example of this process when he recently asked the CEO of one of the largest and most successful retail organizations on earth to identify a moment in his life when he had learned something that profoundly shaped his views on leadership.

The man admitted that he he'd been a lousy student in high school and was barely able to gain entry into a local community college following graduation. The first class he took in college was a history course. On the first day, the professor assigned three books for each student to read and told them to come back to discuss the books in several weeks. The three books were all on the same famous battle.

After reading them, the future business leader came back to class curious as to why they described the same battle in distinctly different ways. The professor indicated that history, like other aspects of life, is simply open to interpretation. The way we view history is based upon our own models and theories of how we view the world. There is that word, "theory," again. So, not only do we have to guess about what will happen and what just happened, we also have to interpret what already happened.

Life's program, looking back, at present, and into the foreseeable future, presents some interesting challenges for all of us. One of the key lessons both the GM plant manager and the CEO in his history class took away with them is that leaders must be able to interpret the past and the present in order to bring the future to the present. They then must go a step further in getting others to interpret what the future in the present looks like. If they're successful, they can create an alignment of purpose targeted toward achieving the future that is already understood in the present.

This somewhat confusing process was clearly demonstrated in the example of the GM plant manager. It also gives clarity to Bruce's observation of the retail giant CEO's interaction with at least four major consulting firms presenting their proposals to his firm. The CEO's theory, at least partly derived from his history class while in college, led him to provide a forum for such an important decision.

Specifically, he required each consultant to offer him a different interpretation of the "same" problem. Then it was up to him to choose, from the different interpretations, which one made the most sense. Indeed, leaders are charged almost daily to make sense out of what has happened, what is happening, and what will happen in the future. Then they bring the event back to the present and get to work on filling in the white space between the present and future. The CEO simply wanted at least three interpretations of the same challenge—a theory he had formulated from a moment that mattered nearly 30 years earlier.

Positive moments contribute to shaping the story of your leadership development potential.

CAPTURING AND FACILITATING MOMENTS

In our view, a key to understanding and developing authentic leadership is capturing these "moments that matter" and that help create positive moments that matter in the future. Some, actually most, of these moments will occur as one walks through life. But for ALD, others can occur because we plan for them to occur. Although both natural and planned moments constitute ALD, in most cases we have ignored life's moments—like the CEO's history class—in our leadership development training efforts. An exception is personal coaching, which may create moments or reflect on ones that have passed; but unfortunately, even then, they are too often not likely to have the intended impact on leadership development.

We have recently been asking a simple question of many leadership developers, senior leaders, and those who run some of the most prestigious leadership learning institutions in the United States, such as the Harvard Business and Kennedy schools, West Point, and the Air Force Academy. The question is: *What is the most significant moment that you've created that accelerates the positive development of leadership?*

Within these well-known institutions, there has been no consensus on what that moment has been or should be. Indeed, most were surprised not to have thought about "that moment," or even "a set of moments," in the design of their leadership curriculum and programs. Those we questioned usually added that they knew such moments exist, but they weren't sure when.

Our challenge to you, and to anyone serious about authentic leadership development, is to consider the "moments that matter" in order to move the future to the present. These will include the ones that you deliberately and proactively set about creating, as wells as the ones that life's program will take care of on its own.

At this point, take some ownership of what you've been reading so far and, after reflection, identify what moment or moments truly mattered in your leadership development. These would be moments that, above all others, you would not want to have missed. Have you created that moment for others?

Now that we hopefully have you at least thinking about your own moments that matter, read on.

SUMMING UP AND POINT OF DEPARTURE

Let's summarize a bit and offer the following basic premises that can be used as a platform and point of departure for your ALD:

- Moments that matter can come from the natural course of life's events or can be proactively created or accelerated for one's self-development and/or that of others.
- Some moments have an immediate impact, and others may take years to surface and have an impact in retrospect or at the point of discovery.
- There are positive moments that matter in the authentic development of leadership, just as there are negative ones.
- Accelerating leadership development requires knowing the terminal learning objective, or TLO, for the creation of moments that matter or for taking advantage of moments as they arise in life. The TLO provides a clear view and, with the resulting moments, a compass for the future.

- ALD will be optimized to the extent that it supports rather than competes with life's program.

In ensuing chapters, we intend to take you through a model that can help shape your theory of what constitutes authentic leadership development. Unless we help you develop and "own" your theory, which is the architectural plan, road map, and compass for your development, there is no way any change in development can be meaningful and sustainable.

In the next chapter, we look at how America views its leaders based on a Gallup Leadership Institute national poll we had conducted for our work on authentic leadership. Our goal is to expand this poll to other countries, so we can build a normative database, one that can serve over time as a basis of comparison for leaders around the globe.

As part of your engagement and ownership, we encourage you to also participate in the poll survey by using the PIN number provided on the cover flap of this book after our bios and going to the survey located at www.e-leading.com. After participating, you will receive an automated feedback report. We have also set up a coaching Web site at e-leading that contains facilities for helping you translate the survey data into some "moments that matter" for you in your development as an authentic leader.

Following the review of the poll data in Chapter 2, in Chapter 3 we summarize what we have learned from the last 100 years of research on virtually any attempt to develop or change leadership. This is the most extensive quantitative review of the leadership development literature ever conducted.

Our brief summary of results is based on a meta-analysis of all relevant studies. Commonly used in the social and health sciences, a meta-analysis is a study of studies, so to speak. This procedure allows us to quantitatively and qualitatively combine data from both published and unpublished studies in order to reach some overall conclusions about what we have actually learned over the last century of research on leadership development interventions.

After laying this unprecedented foundation for how employees across the country view their leaders and what we have learned from the research on leadership interventions, we move on in later chapters to broaden and build on what constitutes authentic leadership development. We will expand our boundaries of this discussion to the global scene, and not limit ourselves simply to a Western view of leadership development.

Our terminal learning objective (TLO) for authentic leadership development for this book is:

> To enhance each reader's personal theory of authentic leadership development in order to have a positive and sustainable impact on self, group, organizational, and community leadership performance.

Once again, we want you to consider a variation of the question asked earlier:

> What moment in your life thus far has had a profoundly positive impact on accelerating your authentic leadership development?

What follows are several examples, the first two drawn from the authors' experiences, of answering this "moments that matter" question.

Bruce's Story

When I was 12 years old, I had a paper route in New York. On my first day, the supervisor allocated routes to all of the newspaper boys. My route was the last to be allocated, and the supervisor for some reason apparently took a dislike to me. I could tell that he had saved this particular route for me.

I got on my bike, headed out to the area where my route began, and realized that a good portion of the route was in the African-American neighborhood of our community, which otherwise was predominantly white. Looking back, there is no doubt in my mind that I was scared, but didn't actually know why. On that day, I delivered the papers and nothing happened. Indeed, nothing happened day after day for two years, except that I got to know some really nice people, who would give me lemonade on hot days, presents on holidays, and who simply went on with their lives, as I did while doing my job. This was 1965, which was a moment in U.S. history where we were on the verge of exploding onto the civil rights scene.

Upon reflection, the moment surrounding my first venture into this neighborhood made me realize that I had heard many false truths about African Americans. My theory of diversity was distorted and incomplete. I was so fortunate to see this large and important group in our nation as uniquely different and diverse in 1965, which has led me over the last 40 years of my life to believe that my theory of leadership is not weighed down by the melanin content of one's skin.

About five years ago a colleague of mine thanked me for sending a candidate for a job his way. He remarked that he was surprised that I had never mentioned that he was African American. My not mentioning it had nothing to do with EEO. It may sound strange to some, but I truly never considered or saw him as an African American. He was just a friend and colleague, and that was the category that worked best for me. It seems, based on reflection and a whole lot of psychological literature on stereotyping, a much more intelligent categorization. I am literally color blind, and consider myself fortunate to be so, at least as far as my "theory" of people goes.

Fred's Story

An especially important moment for me was not only the thrill of my wife Kay giving birth to our first child, Kristin—at the West Point hospital while I was teaching (leadership, no less) while serving in the Army—but a simple comment made by my father when he was informed of the birth: "Freddie, now that you are a father, remember, you only have one chance to do this right, so give it your best shot."

This served as a defining moment that shaped my theory of the importance and the priority that family has for me: my wife of 42 years; four successful and, more important, happy grown children, and their spouses; our six grandchildren (so far); and my sister and other relatives. And it reflected, and reflects, my personal theory of authentic leadership. This theory for me has family, and all that entails, as a central theme—including all the people with whom I deal—with giving, in my father's words, "my best shot."

An Old School Schedule

About six months ago the commissioner of education in a large midwestern state, addressing a think tank composed of superintendents, said that he had recently visited his father's old high school before they were scheduled to tear it down. On a door, he found a schedule of classes that was 50 years old, and remarked that it was very similar to one he had seen recently, except there was a bit more emphasis on Latin! In that moment, we all realized that we had to take a very deep look at educational reform, given how dramatically the world had changed over the last 50 years.

What Did You Accomplish?

Our editor and publisher, of this book, related his own story about his defining leadership moment. Jeffrey Krames, who was born to immigrant parents who never had the chance to attend college, has always been a self-starter. He graduated from college at 20 years of age, and spent more than 20 years working his way up the ladder in the publishing business. He also has written five books in the last five years, nearly all of them best-sellers.

He often wondered where all of that ambition came from. Upon reading this chapter, Jeffrey told us that when he was in his teens and early 20s, his mother would always ask the same question when he returned home from school or a social event: "Well, did you accomplish?"

It was that simple. Those words, and the idea that he needed to accomplish something every day, stayed with him. He awakens every day with that thought in his head, and never considers a day done unless he has achieved something that he deems meaningful.

FOR YOU TO DO ON YOUR ALD JOURNEY

1. Write down what you believe are three core aspects of ideal leadership.
2. Think about how you learned that these were the three core aspects. Where did that knowledge come from? Was it a class/program course? Or was it your life course based on observation and defining moments?
3. How well do these three core aspects apply to your current leader?
4. How satisfied are you with this current leader?
5. Is your level of satisfaction with this leader related to the gap between the three ideals and where your leader operates?

What you have just done is unearth what we said earlier and what leadership academics call your "implicit theory of leadership." Even if you don't think about this personal theory, it's always operating in your head. It acts as a filter as to how you see others, as well as yourself, in terms of leadership. It's very powerful, but subtle. Are you now ready to continue on the journey of your ALD process? As Fred's father would say: Let's give it your best shot!

LEADERSHIP NOTES

- *Even negative experiences can be turned into positive leadership moments.* As we learned at the outset of this chapter, even a negative experience like a heart attack can be used as fodder for a positive leadership experience. Much of the outcome will be determined by how the leader approaches the negative experience. The plant manager at that apparently ill-fated GM plant is a perfect example.
- *Capturing moments that matter is a key component of effective leadership.* One of the keys is to be aware of those moments that made the most impact on your leadership perspective. This may take some real introspection, but it is worth the effort.

Continue to monitor your ALD progress with your journal. Your journal, which we suggested you keep earlier, can be the key to deriving the most value out of the book. Stick with it as you progress through each and every chapter.

2

U.S. POLL ON AUTHENTIC LEADERSHIP

F OR A FEW YEARS now we have been receiving what is called Gallup's Tuesday Briefing. This is a synopsis of Gallup's polling data, as well as the extensive work it has done in areas such as human measurement, performance, and productivity.

On one Tuesday morning, the Gallup pollsters sent out a chart that captured the last 30 years of data on the U.S. public's confidence and trust in its leadership, covering a period from the end of the Vietnam War through the current Iraq War. Surprisingly, the poll data showed that the confidence in business leadership over the past three decades has remained virtually the same.

Specifically, on a scale of 0 to 100, the confidence in business leadership has hovered around 28, right through the bursting of the dot-com bubble at the turn of the present century, through 9/11, and even through the corporate ethics meltdown in recent years. However, one number that has not been steady is the jump in the number of ethics officers appointed in our organizations, which in 2003–2004 has increased 25 percent, according to the Ethics Officer Association.

In a Gallup Poll in 2002, 51 percent of U.S. employees said they agreed that "the people who run most companies are ethical and honest." If 49 percent are not viewed as ethical, our businesses and indeed our democracy may be in serious trouble.

Fortunately, we believe the situation is not so dire. For example, in a 2004 survey of U.S. companies conducted by the Center for Corporate Citizenship at Boston College, 82 percent of companies noted that good corporate citizenship was important to their bottom line. Also, 72 percent said that the public has the right to expect good corporate citizenship. In another survey, the Conference Board notes that 50 percent of global managers report their companies will include citizenship as part of their performance evaluation, or that there are plans to this effect.

During this same 30-year span, from the end of the Vietnam War through the war and occupation in Iraq, the confidence and trust in U.S. military leadership has remained at about 80 out of 100. What is remarkable about both sets of data, besides the stark contrast between the reactions to business versus military leaders, is how little the confidence in leadership has changed over time, despite various events and, from the perspective of our book, moments that mattered. Although we all know about the media blitz and hallway discussions about what has gone wrong with our business leaders, these data representing their brand has not changed over the last 30 years. (Given the low ratings, this consistency is not necessarily a good thing.)

Regarding the military, we wonder how certain widely publicized events in recent years will affect our trust in those leaders as well. For example, a *New York Times* article on November 11, 1998 revealed that the accident that occurred on the Cermis ski lift in the Italian Alps, where a U.S. Marine pilot struck a cable and as a result killed 20 people, was due in part to a lack of transparency. Apparently, critical information for Air Force pilots was "simply dropped in the mailboxes of the Marines," potentially contributing to this tragic accident.

In the May 17, 2004, issue of ArmyTimes.com, under the title "A Failure of Leadership at the Highest Levels," there was a discussion of ethical mistakes made by soldiers who abused prisoners in Afghanistan and in Iraq, at Abu Ghraib. But it lays blame on the conditions on the leadership in the military, all the way to the top, for creating the conditions in which the abuses took place. Seymour Hersh was the first to write about this in mainstream publications, in a three-part article in *The New Yorker* magazine in the same year. What impact will these and other events have on the trust Americans place in our military leaders?

Military leaders remain the most trusted in U.S. society, while business leaders lag way behind in terms of trust and confidence.

THE ROLE OF SELF-SACRIFICE

What makes people more confident in our military leaders versus our business leaders? Why are military leaders likely to be seen as more authentic?

Perhaps the answer to these questions lies in part within the discussions we hear every four years surrounding the qualifications to become President. Two candidates who, approximately, are equally qualified to hold the office try to differentiate (or in some cases hide from) their military records because the voters know they will become Commander in Chief of our armed forces.

This emphasis to gain competitive advantage from one's "war record" gets to one of the most fundamental truths about leadership. It is back to our "moments that matter." There is no better way of demonstrating your authenticity than the willingness to sacrifice your life for a cause, a mission, or, in this case, your fellow soldiers. Clearly, these are challenging moments.

Doing one's regular job may demonstrate steadfast commitment. It may be less notable, to most people, than being a war hero, but it's no less important to one's authenticity, and to how others view it.

To others, self-sacrifice signals your commitment. It may be as simple as waiting in line last to be fed, delaying your vacation to help someone get their project done, evenly splitting the rewards from a successful project, giving up something you value for the good of your group, and/or saying what you think when it most matters, even if it will detract from your career prospects or compensation bonus.

It's Herb Kelleher down in the hold of one of his Southwest planes, helping unload baggage on Christmas day. It is the Westinghouse executive who offered to buy, and then cook and serve, a steak dinner to his direct reports if they met their sales goal, even when the company offered to pay the bill at a fine restaurant. It is the executive who comes to a troubled airline and cuts his salary the first day by 25 percent. Or, it may be the reason why nurses in our country are the highest rated profession in terms of being viewed as ethical and honest, while car salesmen are ranked the lowest, according to a 2004 Gallup Poll.

The lesson to be learned here is: The moment that matters to followers is when the leader shows that her people are more important than she is. In its best form, it is actually enlightened self-interest. Why? Because followers will do much more for leaders who they believe have the followers' interests in mind.

Choosing such self-sacrificing actions is based on moments that matter in the leader's own life, moments that taught him or her that it was the only right thing to do. However, self-sacrifice is only one way to show sincerity and commitment. It is not by any means the only one we will advocate for ALD.

Also, self-sacrifice may have significant drawbacks to one's leadership career, like death in the military or stressful overwork for the rest of us. Nevertheless, in the case of the armed forces, the operating premise for men and women on active duty is that by choosing to serve, they have already demonstrated to us some level of self-sacrifice. They have voluntarily joined an institution that has been draped in self-sacrifice for 250 years. The bottom line is that we trust and attribute authenticity to leaders who sacrifice for the good of others, which is an important lesson to learn in creating moments for yourself and others in your ALD process.

Leaders often gain authenticity through selfless acts that contribute to the good of their respective groups.

CONTRASTING MILITARY AND BUSINESS LEADERS

Let's take this a step further by contrasting the normative view of military leaders with that of business leaders. In every business school, contrary to what we know from psychological theory, business students are taught to think in "quid pro quo" terms: Always strive to get a maximum return on the money you invest.

A popular model taught to business school students, especially on the financial side of the house, is called "agency theory." In a nutshell, this theory essentially says that, as employees, we are all agents working in this larger entity called a business corporation, putting in effort in exchange for what we expect to receive (i.e., wages). Then we witness, highlighted by the media, the huge gaps between what CEOs make and what the lowest paid agents earn in their respective organizations. The ratio between them in this country is often as great as 400 to 1.

Even in down years we see, leaders still getting large bonuses, based on legitimate contractual agreements, while companies might well be suffering their worst losses in history. Recent highly visible examples include Disney's Michael Eisner, who, over a recent five-year period. returned a dismal –41 percent to stockholders, but was paid a whopping $706.1 million over the same period. Or Motorola's Christopher Galvin (grandson of the founder), who also had a –41.6 percent five-year return to stockholders, but was still paid $28.1 million over that same period.

With the public and legal system demanding more accountability of business leaders in the aftermath of the Enron, Tyco, WorldCom, and other business scandals, things seem to be getting better. For example, CEO Donald Carty was recently forced out at American Airlines, largely as a result of failing to mention the special bonus pool that existed for top executives—while at the same time asking flight attendants and pilots to take massive pay cuts.

A recent survey found that over three-fourths of the CEOs at the worst-performing firms in the S&P 500 have been replaced. The concern of the public, reflected in the passage of the Sarbanes-Oxley Act, is holding business leaders' feet to the fire of increased accountability. Unfortunately, however, it is still easier to come up with stories of greed than altruism.

Dennis Kozlowski, Martha Stewart, and others still seem to dominate the news, rather than a Jim Goodnight or Aaron Feuerstein. Jim runs perhaps the best place to work, at SAS, and Aaron paid millions to his nonworking employees—essentially out of his own pocket—when his company, Malden Mills, burned down several years ago. As strategy guru Henry Mintzberg, author of the highly critical book on business leader education, *Managers Not MBAs*, notes: "Enron and the rest of them are the tip of the iceberg, and you can deal with the tip in courts of law. What worries me is the *legal* corruption below the surface." He specifically mentions the extremes of executive compensation, casual downsizing, and what he calls "hired guns applying neutral techniques to whatever needs managing."

Henry's and our point is that too many of these "top guns" are being developed through flawed business educations. We would argue that they too often follow theories such as agency, rather than theories such as self-sacrifice or even rational egoism. Henry says MBAs are not managers. We would add that traditionally educated MBAs do not necessarily make authentic leaders.

Over the last few decades, the agency theory type of thinking taught in business schools has dominated the personal theories of business leaders. We would argue that our own University of Nebraska-Gallup MBA in authentic leadership is an exception, since it challenges the basic assumptions guiding most traditional MBA programs. (Our Web site, www.gli.unl.edu, presents the details of this program.)

What this all means is that perceptions of authentic leadership is lower in business than in other leadership domains, such as the military. For example, regardless of your feelings about the Iraq War, in terms of accountability, trust, and effectiveness of dollars spent by the leader, who would you choose in comparing General Tommy Franks spending $63 billion in leading his troops to Baghdad versus CEO Rick Wagoner's $175 billion annual spending in leading General Motors?

Is the base rate for authentic leadership inherently lower in business?

WHAT CAN BUSINESS LEADERS DO?

To the extent that leadership is in large part how one is perceived, then the most authentic business leaders will need to demonstrate, through consistent action and visible self-sacrifice, that they value the people with whom they work. They must show that they place their people over their own self-interests in moments where leadership really matters.

One business leader facing closure of his company described reaching back to such a moment when he stated: "Through the whole crisis, I continued to tell myself that I wasn't a quitter. I spent four years through the plebe system at the Citadel and graduated, and I wasn't going to let this beat me. I guess it is just the inner man that makes you survive." And many authentic leaders have indeed drawn from their inner strengths, showing the belief in themselves—and in their people—that make business enterprises not only survive, but flourish.

We would suggest that in today's hypercompetitive environment, most top business leaders already sacrifice a great deal for the good of their companies. In truth, few, if any, have a life outside of leading their organizations. There is little time left for family or friends, let alone leisure activities.

As one business leader put it: "Work weeks of 120 hours take their toll on a family . . . We survived, but we're scarred." However, such hard work, dedication, and commitment to others on the part of many still appears to be overshadowed by the overall perception that business leaders are not trustworthy to lead our corporations.

There is also evidence, from the international study on Global Leadership and Organizational Effectiveness, simply known as the GLOBE project that cultural differences do affect leaders' values and what others expect of them. This massive study includes data from about 17,000 mostly middle level business leaders from 825 organizations in 61 countries.

The GLOBE study found business leaders from southern Asian, Latin American, and Arab countries tend to place a high value on collective goals; that they encourage and reward group distribution of resources and rewards, and express pride, loyalty, and cohesiveness in their organizations and families. In contrast, business leaders from Nordic European countries tend to place a high value on individual goals (more "me" focused). These Nordic values are more in line with U.S. business leaders' values and how others view them.

Leadership is in large part driven by how others perceive you. Do they trust your intentions? Are they confident in your capacity to lead? Do they believe you even know who they are?

In 2004 we decided to start a poll on authentic business leadership. Our intent was, and is, to conduct this poll every other year, to better determine what it is that Americans trust in their business leaders. We didn't set out to discover if our business leaders are more or less ethical or moral. Rather, we set out to collect data on American's perceptions of their business leaders' authenticity, and to present the data for you to be the judge.

Most would agree that the majority of business leaders are honest and ethical, but also perhaps too self-interested at the expense of others. Moreover, one of the real problems we see is that most CEOs want to hear the good news, not the bad. In so doing, they create the conditions that result in their not knowing what might be going on in their own organizations.

Part of the problem is that most people who report to the leader may also overestimate the extent to which their leaders see their inner feelings as transparent, when in fact they are not. So the leader creates the conditions to learn less, and the followers believe that the leader is in fact telling them more than he or she is, which in combination is a recipe for potential disaster.

HOW OUR POLL WAS CONDUCTED

The nationwide telephone poll of 1,008 employees over age 18 was conducted in May to early, June 2004, by the Gallup Organization for the College of Business Administration at the University of Nebraska. Responses to the items comprising the poll were judged on a five-point scale to determine how frequently the leaders of the respondents' respective organizations displayed specific actions and behaviors associated with authentic leadership.

For the poll, we defined authentic leaders as being "transparent" about their intentions and desires. Authentic leaders were also defined as saying exactly what they mean, as going beyond self-interest for the good of the organization, and as acting in the organization's best interest. Further, they consider the moral and ethical consequences of their decisions, and readily admit when mistakes are made.

Many leaders from the past have tended to operate with a guarded, top-down decision-making style. This approach is simply not acceptable in today's organizations. The standard now should be that anything one does in a leadership role should be justifiable and open to public scrutiny. As Warren Buffett is well known for saying, every action you take should be an acceptable headline the next morning in the *New York Times,* a headline you would not be embarrassed to have your family and friends read.

Put bluntly, in today's environment, if leaders aren't transparent and trustworthy, they're eventually going to be caught. We believe that few will be able to get away with the kind of unethical behavior we have seen in the recent past.

The odds are now in favor of leaders being more transparent. Why? There's more noise. There is much more scrutiny from all levels. The media is smarter and more aggressive, at least in the realm of financial reporting. Everyone is currently open to review by everyone else, including—and perhaps more important than the legal system and the media—the leaders' associates. Followers, peers, and even outsiders, such as customers and vendors, are much smarter and more vigilant than in the past.

One follower can now "Google" you into submission with just a touch of the keyboard. A message from one employee can be sent to thousands inside or outside the organization, igniting a movement, ruin a career, or simply getting a bunch a people to show up (in person or online) to voice their opinions.

Today's stark reality is that leaders need to either ramp up their deviousness, or give up and be transparent. A transparency strategy is the only alternative in today's litigious, networked world. To put it cynically, you might as well be transparent and ethical, since people are too smart not to find out when you're being unethical. Thus, it's the practical alternative. From an authentic perspective, a society and economy is based on openness and trust, which is what we advocate for business leaders.

In today's environment, leaders have to operate with employees on the basis of trust. They have to create the conditions for trust in order for their people to flourish and build a sustainable high-performing organization.

Without building the conditions for deep trust, the leader, associates, and the organization can never achieve full potential. Hence, over time, leaders who continually pass the trust test with their authenticity will not only accrue enormous goodwill inside and outside the organization, but also higher performing associates and the resulting competitive advantage.

WHAT OUR LEADERSHIP POLL FOUND

At this point, let us briefly summarize the results of our Gallup Poll on authentic leadership:

- Approximately one-third of U.S. working adults indicated that the leadership in their organizations exhibited authentic behaviors "frequently, if not always."
- Thirty-nine percent of the employees surveyed reported that their leaders frequently, if not always "act in the best interest of the organization" and "are genuine people."
- The lowest-rated items from the poll were leaders who "make personal sacrifices for the benefit of the organization"—only 22 percent said "frequently, if not always"—and "admits when mistakes are made," with only 23 percent reporting that their leaders exhibit this behavior frequently, if not always.

The survey also separated responses by gender, and white versus nonwhite. Women respondents typically had more positive views of their organization's leadership, and nonwhites had a somewhat less positive view than whites.

The poll also revealed that employees in smaller organizations (of less than 100 employees) were more likely to rate their leaders as displaying authentic leadership. Perhaps in larger organizations it is more difficult to sustain authentic leadership because people are less likely to know the leader or CEO personally. They may only know what they've heard secondhand from others or read in the external press or internal publications. Or they may have had only a brief moment of informal—or worse, very formal—interaction with the leader, from which they had to shape their opinion. Besides these major findings from the poll, here are some other interesting findings to ponder:

- One-fourth of women versus 16 percent of men felt their organizations picked the best people for leadership roles "frequently, if not always."
- Thirty-nine percent of women, versus 27 percent of men, indicated their leaders highlighted the advantages of working with people from different backgrounds "frequently, if not always."
- About one-fourth (26 percent) of white employees, versus one out of five nonwhite employees, indicated "frequently, if not always" that their organization's leadership makes them feel like an owner in their organization.
- Almost half (48 percent) of the white employees indicated that their leadership gave them significant freedom to do their job "frequently, if not always," versus 35 percent for nonwhites.
- About one-third (34 percent) of those employed in small

organizations (less than 100) indicated that their leaders made them feel like an owner in their organization "frequently, if not always," versus approximately 18 percent in medium to larger organizations.

- Not quite a third (31 percent) of those employed in smaller organizations indicated that their leaders pick the best people for leadership roles "frequently, if not always," versus approximately 14 percent in medium to larger organizations.
- Well over half (56 percent) of the respondents from small organizations indicated that their leaders give them significant freedom to do their jobs "frequently, if not always," versus 38 percent in medium to larger organizations.
- Not quite two-thirds (63 percent) from small organizations indicated their leaders make them feel their work makes an important contribution to the mission of their organization "frequently, if not always," versus 45 percent in medium to larger organizations.

IMPLICATIONS FOR ALD FROM THE POLL RESULTS

The pattern of results associated with small versus large organizations has important implications for ALD. Specifically, leadership in a smaller organization or unit versus a larger organization may require a different approach. Much of how you are perceived as a leader in a large organization will depend on the "moments that mattered" to your employees in shaping their views of your leadership. Especially in larger organizations, where there are less direct day-to-day personal interactions, impression management takes on added importance.

It is at the intersection of impression management and actual observed behavior that the followers formulate or confirm their perceptions of leadership. The following mostly widely publicized examples underscore this point:

- When former President Clinton, intensely stared into the camera and told the American public that he did not have a sexual relationship with "that woman," Monica Lewinsky, it was a defining moment for many Americans, but not all, on his character. Many already questioned his character, and this statement and its aftermath just reaffirmed their view of his lack of authenticity. Others did not view personal affairs as having any relevance to public affairs, so they simply dismissed it.
- Shane Osborne courageously landing his plane on an island off the coast of China after being hit by a Chinese fighter jet was a defining moment for this young officer in the eyes of the American public. This new hero brought his crew down safely, but the general public did not know that previously he had 22 other similar so-called bad incidents where he had to undertake risky landings. It was this defining moment in China that mattered to the American public regarding his authentic leadership. Interestingly, this event also became a moment for George W. Bush's leadership because he was addressing his first major international incident as President.
- When Martha Stewart publicly derided the court system as unfair following her conviction for insider trading, it reinforced the moment that rich CEOs and celebrities want to be treated with different standards from the rest of us, whether she was in fact guilty or not.
- President Nelson Mandela positioning the four guards who kept him captive over the years in the front row at his inaugural acceptance speech and shaking their hands first as he ascended the stage was a major moment for the healing process in his beleaguered country.

■ Eleanor Roosevelt first heard of her husband's death in Warm Springs, Georgia, and then discovered that he was with the woman whom he continued to have an affair with for over 20 years. She nevertheless attended to the funeral arrangements with dignity and grace, reinforcing the public's confidence that the country would be okay in the midst of ending World War II. Several months later, she found a sketch of a portrait FDR was having done for this mistress at the time of his death. Eleanor chose to send it to the mistress because she knew how much it would mean to her. Eleanor did not allow her anger to consume her enormous capacity to show goodwill toward "all people" on earth. She realized that this woman loved FDR too, and that's what drove her decision.

■ After giving a keynote speech to a large group of real estate agents and brokers, Colin Powell was asked the off-the-wall question: "General Powell, I understand that your wife once suffered from depression, had to take medicine, and was even in a mental hospital. Do you want to comment on that?" Everyone was aghast, and you could hear a pin drop as they awaited his answer. In this defining moment for himself, and for how others perceived him, Powell replied: "Excuse me sir, the person you love more than anyone is living in hell, and you don't do whatever you can to get her out? Do you have a problem with that, sir?" The journalist who observed this exchange declared, "You felt Powell's values and principles fuse into deeply felt conviction. Talk about leadership! I said to myself, 'I would buy a used country from that guy.'"

■ The owner of a large construction company decided to retire and sell his business. He did so for a huge profit, and provided his workforce with excellent benefits for their transition. Then he cut each employee a check, making them all instant millionaires—not because he had to, but because he felt that without them, the company that had made him so prosperous was not truly a company in the real sense of the word. Everyone marveled at the quality of his workforce, and he paid them in the end for all they did to build the trust others had in "their business."

■ A university chancellor had to make significant cuts in the budget three years running. At the start of his tenure as chancellor he set in motion the idea that the university would build on its spires of excellence even in down years. So, under pressure, but with faculty input, he cut a few tenured faculty positions in low priority areas while supporting the hiring of new faculty in areas of excellence. As a reaction to cutting tenured faculty, the head of the faculty senate called for a vote of no confidence in the chancellor, but this occurred toward the end of the year, when it was too late to actually implement, and so it was delayed until the fall. Within a week, the chancellor sent out an announcement that he'd contracted with the head of the State Election Commission to conduct the vote on whether he should stay or go. He put it all on the line in this unofficial vote, and the subsequent vote among both faculty and staff was over 90 percent in favor of him doing what he had stated he would. The chancellor retained his position.

Such authentic acts of leadership acts create powerful moments for shaping how we perceive our leaders, and perhaps how they in turn view us. One CEO we know described her father's advice to her as follows: "Lynn, you know when you are on the thin white bright line and when you are off, and that is what should guide your decision."

Apparently, there are a considerable number of leaders in large and small, public and private, organizations in the United States who actually do know when they are on the "thin white bright line" and act accordingly. Even through it can appear nebulous, we would argue that most kids, let alone business leaders, indeed know what is the "right thing" to do in various "gray" ethical situations.

Recently, Warren Buffett came to the University of Nebraska, his alma mater, to teach a class on leadership. He had much to say about ethics and business, most of which he himself admitted came merely from his common good "midwestern" sense of values and upbringing.

He talked about a letter he wrote to the CEOs of Berkshire Hathaway companies that he usually sent out once every two years. It didn't change much from year to year because it simply reaffirmed the importance of ethics and business. The letter started something like: "It has taken 37 years for our company to be ranked as one of the most admired in the world by *Fortune* magazine, and it could take a mere 37 seconds to destroy it all."

Buffett then relayed a discussion he'd just had on the way down to the university with John Gutfreund, former chairman of Solomon Brothers, and a recently acquired Wall Street firm. He told the students that Gutfreund had appeared on the cover of *Business Week* with an article entitled, "King of Wall Street." Several months after being anointed king, Gutfreund stepped down amidst one of the worst scandals in recent times. The incident involved a rather simple but inappropriate action taken by a Solomon trader who Gutfreund decided not to go public on, until the same trader did it again.

Buffett said something else that set the bar in terms of trust and authenticity. In response to a student's question about how he defined success, he said it was based on how many people would "hide you" if their life and yours depended on it.

It happens that this unusual but profound answer was inspired by an elderly and successful businesswoman in Omaha who had survived the Holocaust as a young girl. She told Buffett that you should consider yourself successful in life based on those who will hide you. He joked that most of the rich people he knew would not even include their kids on the list of people who would hide them.

The high bar for success in life may be how many people love you enough to hide you.

This life success criterion hit particularly close to home for Bruce. Though his last name is Avolio, his mother's maiden name is Greenspan, and her mother and father were the only family members to leave Germany in time to survive the Holocaust. After hearing Warren Buffett, Bruce was on a long drive with his wife Beth, during which they discussed who would hide them—including their children. When Bruce now defines an enduring relationship, he can't help but think about whether the person whom he considers his very special friend or family member would, in the moment that mattered, not just defend and protect him, but hide him at personal sacrifice and danger.

In a presentation given to the National Academy of Management in Washington, D.C., Bruce mentioned this "hiding criterion" of one's life success to an audience of approximately 150 scholars and practitioners. About a month later he received an e-mail from a student who had attended the meeting and indicated that, like Bruce, he was the grandchild of people who had survived the Holocaust. Bruce's remarks had led him to think deeply about his relationships as well. Isn't it amazing how one moment can multiply in effect across time, people, and situations?

We wonder how many of the leaders who received "frequently, if not always" on the questions in our Gallup Poll regarding the willingness to sacrifice for the good of their people have a good, solid list of people who would hide them. We think those who could count on this are certainly more authentic than the leaders who could not come up with such a list.

FOR YOU TO DO ON YOUR ALD JOURNEY

1. Go to the Web site www.e-leading.com and sign in to take the survey poll on authentic leadership.
2. You will be asked to identify up to five individuals who know you well enough to complete the survey you just completed.
3. Insert their e-mails into the list, and once you exit the site, they will receive an e-mail indicating they have been chosen by you to complete this survey.
4. The people you choose to rate you will not be identified in the feedback report you'll receive, and they will be assured of that in the e-mail they receive. Only aggregate feedback will be provided, plus your own ratings.
5. Once you receive the feedback, you will be able to compare your ratings and theirs to the national poll data. Keep in mind that leadership is an interpretation based in part on what we called your implicit theory of leadership and their implicit theory.
6. We like to say that everyone's perception of your leadership is accurate and real. It is their perception, after all, and therefore how they are viewed and interpreted by their raters in terms of their leadership actions *and* their implicit theory of leadership. The same, of course, is true of your ratings.
7. At the Web site, you will be provided with some additional information on how to interpret the report, and what to do with it in terms of creating a "moment that mattered."

LEADERSHIP NOTES

- *It appears to be more difficult to lead authentically in larger versus smaller organizations.* To make sure people in your organization perceive you as an authentic, high impact leader, you must be aware of how to use the positive moments that matter in your interactions with them. Assume every moment matters in enhancing trust.

- *The base rate for trusting business leaders is much lower than other professions, such as the military.* The advantage of being a business leader is that you can elevate people's expectations of you as a business leader by being transparent, making choices for the good of your followers whenever possible, and showing some self-sacrifice.

A note of caution: You need to consider what constitutes genuine leadership in different cultures, since there are different behaviors and styles that will generate more or less trust in different places. It is important to know these differences. One way to find out is by asking the most admired managers/leaders who work in that culture.

3

100 YEARS LATER, WHAT DO WE REALLY KNOW ABOUT LEADERSHIP DEVELOPMENT?

L ESS THAN TWO YEARS ago a new doctoral program with a specific focus on leadership was initiated at the University of Nebraska. Bruce is the founding director of the program and the Gallup Leadership Institute, or GLI. We both serve in the institute, whose mission is to advance the science and practice of authentic leadership development.

Our aspiration is to become the "Bell Labs" for leadership development research. Every research project and doctoral dissertation would be directly or indirectly concerned with advancing the science of what we defined at the outset of the book as authentic leadership development, or ALD.

With our initial dozen doctoral students assembled, we charged them with the following specific research question: Do leadership interventions matter? And, as part and parcel to this question: What do we know based on the last 100 years of work on leadership development?

Thousands of hours later and numerous revisions to the first, second, and then third round of coding, the GLI associates were able to identify 201 studies—out of approximately 3,000—that had systematically evaluated whether leadership interventions matter. In fact, even these 201 used minimally acceptable scientific criteria to test whether leadership interventions mattered.

We used a meta-analytic technique as introduced in the first chapter. Meta-analysis facilitates the compiling of data reported in individual studies into one study, providing a quantitative summary of the overall results. As we indicated, essentially, this meta-analysis is like a literature review, except you accumulate data points, as well as the review, to come up with an aggregate of what we know about leadership development.

In other words, rather than relying on opinion or anecdotal evidence, as almost all leadership books do—even those that depend on a favorable study here or there to support the author's position— our meta-analysis was a quantitative summary of *all* the published leadership intervention studies ever conducted, and a number of unpublished ones as well, that met the minimal scientific inclusion criteria. The results indicate the average relationship between x and y across all leadership intervention studies, or the average difference between treatment A versus treatment B.

As we stated in our introduction, our reason for going back 100 years with this project was to bring the past into the present so we could eventually bring the future back to the present. How? First, we wanted to learn what others had tried. Specifically, we were curious as to what worked or didn't work, and with whom they tried it, including leaders and followers.

We felt it made a lot more sense to build from this most comprehensive research base than to "discover" insights haphazardly or serendipitously along the way. We were confident the insights from this systematic review would lay the foundation for future inquiries we would pursue as an institute and for the methods that would eventually be tested. At this point, we feel that we know the past from the results of the meta-analysis and that our vision for the future can now be brought to the present, which will comprise the rest of this chapter.

HIGHLIGHTS FROM THE META-ANALYSIS

We present first some of the pertinent highlights of this meta-analytic study. However, for readers more interested in the specific details, a full report of the study can be found at the Web site www.gli.unl.edu. This is the "virtual home" of the Gallup Leadership Institute at the University of Nebraska. Here are some of the major findings:

- There are an accelerating number of studies that engage in interventions. These involve research on what we might call the higher end or new genre theories of leadership. They include those that are charismatic, visionary, and transformational. Indeed, there have been 113 intervention studies done since 1990, while the remaining 88 occurred over the preceding 90-year period. We should learn more about the "higher end/higher impact" aspects of leadership regarding what works faster if this trend continues into the future.
- Across all studies, the accumulated evidence indicates that trying to change leadership through an intervention and its impact does have an effect, albeit small. If the effects were random, the positive impact of a leadership intervention would be a probability of 50 percent, or a toss of the coin. But the meta-analysis found the probability of a positive impact was 63 percent across all studies. This effect is not large, but certainly better than chance alone, and therefore meaningful. This impact of the intervention holds across all studies, types of settings, theories, and measures. However,

certain theories or methods do have a larger impact than others and are higher than the average.

- We were amazed to discover that the longest intervention study we were able to uncover was only seven days in length.

- Comparing U.S. based studies to those conducted outside the United States—a little over two-thirds were U.S. based—we found little difference in terms of the impact of the leadership intervention.

- Thus far, some of the greatest effects were seen in a line of research that has tested what is called the "Pygmalion," or Self-Fulfilling Prophecy, Effect. Essentially, half of the leader subjects in these studies were told they would be working with a group of people who were better—usually meaning smarter—more motivated, and so forth. In fact, the groups in these studies were randomly assigned to each leader and did not differ at all. Yet these leaders in the experiments apparently came to believe their followers were indeed different, and guess what—the followers actually performed differently. The so-called smarter or more motivated groups do better if the leader believes they are smarter or more motivated! Ironically, by creating a ruse (which, of course, is inauthentic), the largest leadership intervention effects were obtained, compared to all other methods.

- Generally, we found the effects were greater in more controlled interventions, such as in a lab, versus conducting the work in the field or the real world. One of the laments of many leadership trainers and participants is that "this sounds good in theory" but when I get back to my job it probably won't work. This, of course, refers to the old transfer-of-training bugaboo. We now have some evidence to support this assertion. Our findings suggest we better pay attention and focus on developing the context in which we want to embed new leadership stories, theories, interventions, or whatever you want to call them.

■ We found that although some of the more traditional leadership theories that focused on enhancing old participative or even more directive type leadership had a positive impact, it was generally not as great as those guided by the higher-end leadership models focusing on transformational, charismatic, or visionary leadership.

Overall, we made some discoveries from this extensive meta-analysis that should help guide us in not only the research work we pursue, but also in how we create moments that matter in accelerating ALD. For example, if given the option, there is no doubt that we would take the seven days available in the longest intervention found in our review, but spread those seven days out over the year.

We are also now convinced that probably one of the best places to start leadership development is readying the playing field or home turf (i.e., the context that academics talk about). The new theory has to be brought back into the context so that leadership development can stick.

To sum up, we discovered it is not just being "self-aware" that matters to ALD, or just the intention and understanding of how to change. Such self-awareness and the motivation and knowledge to change are obviously necessary, but, based on our findings, may not be sufficient for effective ALD. The research told us what seems to count is where (i.e., the context) one brings that awareness, motivation, and knowledge. Whether one will be successful in bringing the future leadership development aspiration goal back to the present depends on developing the process in the appropriate context.

The largest development impact was raising the positive beliefs of followers, instilling in them the conviction that they were better at a performance task than they thought.

OTHER SUPPORTING RESEARCH STUDIES

Recently, several well-conceived studies have shown that leadership interventions can have a positive impact on both the ratings of leadership and the group's performance. For example, in a Canadian study, the researchers focused on developing transformational leadership in a short awareness workshop with supervisors, with follow-up leadership development planning. The researchers found the leaders who were trained to be more transformational were seen by their followers over time as indeed more transformational.

This type of research shows that if we can help leaders become more aware of their leadership, they can apparently alter the way they interact with followers, and in turn influence followers to evaluate them differently as leaders.

In what is called a "true field experiment," where the participants were randomly assigned to alternative training conditions, another especially relevant research study found that Israeli platoon commanders trained to be more transformational were evaluated as such by their soldiers over time. Behaving in a more transformational manner positively impacted the motivational levels of soldiers in the trained leader's platoons. Most important, after a six-month period, the performance of these platoons improved.

Although there are many other examples of leadership research using interventions, we chose these two to convey some important lessons regarding the type of future work we are doing and hope to see evolve for ALD.

- We are convinced that even short leadership interventions can positively impact styles of leadership, especially if "boosted" over time with additional follow-up training, facilitation, or coaching. Where we need to distinguish future leadership development work is in areas that many feel are not trainable, or at least that are difficult to train. These areas especially relevant to ALD would include leaders' and followers' values/

beliefs, ethical and moral perspective, positive psychological capital (e.g., confidence, hope, optimism, and resiliency), building trust, willingness to self-sacrifice, future focus, and so on. The attention given to transformational leadership in the studies cited above is beginning to move into these domains of interest to ALD. This is where we believe some of the greatest gains to bring the future to the present will accrue.

- We need to encourage more experimentation—shootouts, if you will—by testing one approach versus another to learn what works best. There are way too many untested assumptions that prevail in the leadership development arena. In fact, this state of affairs results in a lowering of authenticity of leadership developers. Specifically, there is a tendency to present to today's organizations "the" method that will work to enhance leadership effectiveness. Let's be clear: Right now, very few can make such a claim, at least *based on science*. You can go to www.gli.unl.edu for updates to see who is doing the due diligence to make those claims. Why can't corporations partner with consultancies and universities to test out what works, or what works faster and better? We are heavy on curriculum design and presentation style, and light on evaluation of impact.

- Related to the previous point, we would like to put forth a standard for all leadership development programs. What we are advocating is that all leadership development interventions determine the design of the training to estimate the "return on development," or ROD. If you are investing x dollars in developing leaders, what is the expected return? Business leaders use calculations of ROI (return on investment) in making decisions and judging impact. Why not use ROD for leadership development decisions and evaluating impact. As noted in the meta-analytic results above, with a 63 versus 50 percent success rate, we can objectively estimate what the probable return on investment would be for dollars invested in leadership

development. We are suggesting that you "don't spare measuring the ROD" and spoil the opportunity to advance the
science *and* practice of leadership development.

- As stated in Chapter 1, a starting point for ALD is to know
your terminal learning objective, or TLO, and its intended
performance impact points up front. Also, you must have a
way of evaluating whether you've been able to achieve TLO
over time with your intervention. Here are 10 easily measured
impact points for ALD:
   1. Did the leader change how he viewed himself?
   2. Did the leader change the way she viewed the potential
      of her followers?
   3. Did the leader change his behavior toward followers?
   4. Did followers change the way they thought about the
      leader?
   5. Did followers change the way they thought about them-
      selves?
   6. Did followers change their behavior?
   7. How did the leader and followers approach their tasks
      differently?
   8. How did the changes in both the leader and followers
      impact early indicators of success—variables that predict
      changes in short- to long-term performance?
   9. How did performance change as a consequence of the
      intervention?
   10. To what extent was the change in performance stabilized
       across two time periods?
- Consider that in the meta-analysis reported at the beginning
of the chapter nearly two-thirds of the studies used college
students as subjects. Therefore, most of what we know about
leadership development is based on young, or sometimes
called "emerging," adults, generally without full-time work
experience. And what we do know here is that it's likely eas-

ier to shape how young people view their leadership versus those who are further along in their life course. This is simply because young people's "installed base or platform" is not as well-established. Specifically, when someone comes to a workshop in their mid-40s, they have had 40 years to learn through "life's leadership development program." What makes us think that in one to seven days we will change that sufficiently enough to get our desired ROD? We're not suggesting that we cannot effect change, even significant change. This change was indicated in the 100-year review of the leadership intervention literature. What we are suggesting is that we must become much smarter in how we use the training and development days we have. We would argue once again that the smartest starting point is to know the future impact point you want to bring to the present.

When starting a leadership development intervention, know your impact point.

THE BORN VS. MADE ISSUE

It is almost impossible to leave any discussion of leadership development without making some reference to the "born versus made" question. No facilitator in leadership development has ever gotten through more than several workshops or sessions, if not just a couple of hours, without being asked, "Aren't leaders born to lead?"

It strikes us as being a curious question coming from participants already enrolled in leadership development workshops. Are they there to simply watch those "born" leaders get better? Do they view themselves as a born leader, and this as simply a brush-up session? Or are they there because they were told to be there. They are reaffirming in their mind that the person who gave the order to attend is simply wasting their time.

In any event, this born versus made question is legitimate, and has no doubt become part of what we called earlier one's "implicit model" of leadership. Our experience over the years has been that no less than a third, and up to two-thirds, of large groups will raise their hand when asked the question, "How many believe leaders are born rather than made?" It's interesting, however, that no one can accurately answer this question based on solid scientific work.

There has never been a study comparing, say, identical twins trained and untrained in leadership, to see whether they evolve differently from birth. However, we are now beginning to see links made between predispositions toward leadership (e.g., high energy), as well as other personality attributes. Thus, to the extent that more energetic people emerge and excel at taking the lead in groups, we can say that leadership is at least partially born into leaders.

Some more direct research on this issue of born versus made has been recently conducted by two different groups examining identical and fraternal twin pairs. By using twins, the researcher can estimate how much of the commonality in genes for identical twins, which are the same, and fraternal twins, which are approximately 50 percent similar, accounts for differences observed in their leadership.

In a study conducted with a Canadian sample of twins, the researchers reported that self-rated transformational leadership had more of a genetic component than transactional leadership. Nearly 40 percent of the leader's transformational self-ratings could be accounted for by genetics, meaning that there was more commonality with identical versus fraternal twins in their self-perceptions of transformational leadership.

A more recent study, conducted with a sample of twins from the well-known University of Minnesota database, examined the degree to which the emergence of twins in leadership roles was a function of commonalities in genetics. In this study, the researchers examined the degree to which genetics accounted for the emergence of leadership roles in high school, the community, and at work.

In summarizing their findings, the researchers in this study estimated that almost a third (30 percent) of the emergence in leadership roles could be accounted for by genetics with men, with a similar percentage associated with women. In other words, like the previous study using the Canadian twins, if one identical twin emerges as a leader, so will the other to some degree, at least better than chance alone, but obviously not one-to-one or 100 percent of the time.

What this still preliminary research shows is that genetics does play some role in explaining who emerges as a leader in organizations, schools, communities, and government. Yet, how people's genetic endowment interacts with and engages their environment could be considered a "holy grail" explanation of what constitutes ALD success.

In other genetics work, we already know that how a person's genetic makeup engages and is affected by its environment is not stable. Instead, the genetic-environment interaction is elastic (i.e., changes) over time. Specifically, as the "genetic program" unfolds, it is greatly affected by the context in which it unfolds.

The environmental context matters as to how the genetic program plays out. We know that certain genes are triggered into action depending on the characteristics of the context in which the individual lives. For example, someone prone to heart disease will have it triggered by a pattern of living (i.e., context) that promotes such disease. While another individual with essentially the same genetic disposition toward heart problems may either delay or never experience its full effects because of the better environment in which he embeds himself over time.

This discussion reminds us of something Father Flanagan said when he established Boys Town in Omaha, Nebraska, to help kids in trouble. Although genetics researchers have found some evidence linking generations to bad behavior, Father Flanagan (not Spencer Tracy) suggested that we didn't have bad boys, just the conditions that created such behavior. Psychobiology would say that to a great extent he was right, although the genetics are still in place to potentially steer the child in the wrong direction.

Genetics plays an important role in leadership development, but its role is limited to how an individual engages life's program.

THE ROLE OF TRIGGER MOMENTS

Besides the born versus made or nature versus nurture issue that has been ongoing in psychology over the years, what does this all have to do with leadership development? In the model of ALD we have presented so far, and will do a "deeper dive" into the model in the chapters that follow, we maintain that "moments matter."

We will now add to this special moments idea what we call "trigger moments." What we mean by this term is that certain situations will trigger reflections, ideas, emotions, and reactions or behaviors that will contribute to ALD. These trigger moments are essentially what we mean by leadership interventions in the ALD process. Trigger moments may last just several seconds or minutes, or they can be quite long in duration, unfolding gradually over time.

How we trigger ALD (i.e., set up interventions in the process) is essential to achieving the 10 impact points that we suggested a bit earlier as being desirable for growth and performance. Going back to the born versus made issue, if you systematically study well-known leaders, you will find patterns in their development that were triggered by certain moments. In some instances, trigger moments appear to be a brief but consequential interaction. Such a trigger moment later shapes leaders' thinking about who they are and what they want to accomplish.

An often cited example of such trigger moments was Ghandi going to South Africa and for the first time experiencing up close and personal the ugly underbelly of racial discrimination. This trip not only triggered his efforts to liberate his home country of India from domination by the British, but also triggered him concerning the value of a nonviolent strategy. And the nonviolent strategy used by Ghandi also became a full-circle moment for Nelson Mandela to use in South Africa, and by Dr. Martin Luther King in the U.S. civil rights movement.

Such trigger moments do not have to be such monumental historical events. Practice leaders for the Center for Creative Leadership recently told of a senior executive—we'll call her Jane—who was experiencing increasing difficulties with her CEO. While attending a top level executive meeting, right in front of her the CEO blurted, "What are we going to do about our problem with Jane?" Everyone sat in silence, and Jane was embarrassed and dumbfounded. However, for her this humiliating experience served as a trigger moment. In her words, she "reassessed both my career and myself in a way that I'd never done before." Voluntarily, she soon left this firm after landing a CEO position in another company, and experienced great satisfaction (and probably a bit of revenge) in leading her new firm to growth and success.

These trigger moments pop up in life's course and shape the leaders we eventually observe, and whom we wonder whether they were born or made. The answer has to be both born *and* made.

Genetics may predispose the authentic leadership of a Ghandi, Mandela, King, or Jane Doe, but we maintain that the trigger moments then shaped what they pursued, how they pursued it, and with whom they pursued it. These trigger moments help bring the future to the present, and they can be both positive or negative.

A middle-class student from the United States goes on a mission trip with her church to El Salvador. What most strikes her is how much hope they all brought to the township they visited, but how little they did to achieve such hope. She thinks about the little things that build hope each and every day as a consequence of her moment. How will this trigger moment effect her in 20 years?

When Bruce first came to Nebraska, the CEO of Gallup said to him, "A lot of people build great things, but great and different is the winning combination." Since that moment, Bruce has talked with the people in GLI about being different and the best at what we do.

Finally, just imagine the following true story.

When Saddam Hussein's mother was seven months pregnant with him, she unsuccessfully tried to abort the fetus. Once he was born, he was openly rejected by her for the first three years of his life. Saddam was relegated to an uncle who reputedly abused him. Regardless of genetic makeup, we know that the early moments of maternal bonding and the early years of upbringing are critical to triggering a healthy social development of human beings. During these periods we begin to form our healthy attachment to loved ones and humanity in general.

The role of a loving mother is central to healthy development. One does not have to speculate too far as to what these early trigger events did for Saddam's view of humanity and his leadership of the people of Iraq. If a mother does not care for a child in the deepest sense, it may be an almost unrecoverable trigger event in a leader's development, unless a significant alternative is provided to replace the mother. Good luck!

We know of one CEO of a large high technology company who described his parents as always challenging him to the nth degree in everything. However, when he failed, they simply looked at what he had done, explored how to improve his performance, and said try it again. In such challenging and deep support, one may see the beginning of resiliency being developed.

FOR YOU TO DO ON YOUR ALD JOURNEY

1. Think about some traits or characteristics you have observed in your immediate or extended family and how they apply to

your behavior and actions. For example, in some families there seems to be a "thrill-seeking" tendency that runs through family members. They may express this through participating in extreme sports activities more than the average family.

2. As you get older, you begin to see "things" that you have taken from your parent or parents. What is the single most important quality that seems to come from your parents? When did you notice that you noticed?

3. Try to uncover times where your parents discussed things about your development, and determine how that discussion shaped the way you look at yourself with respect to the attributes uncovered in the previous point.

4. Do you see any patterns between what they were trying to teach you to be and what you have turned out to be? How much of the teaching, over the genetics they passed on to you, impacted who you are *becoming*?

5. If you have read a biography recently, go back and take a look at the "early life sections of the book," then skim forward to see whether the leaders describe themselves in ways that link back to those early characteristics shaped by parents, other family members, friends, teachers, etc. Look for linkages between what happened early and what happened late in this person's life, as you have done for yourself.

6. What have you learned about the balance of life's program with the balance of what happens to you in life in terms of shaping your full authentic leadership potential?

LEADERSHIP NOTES

- *At the start of any leadership development intervention, begin by identifying your performance impact point.* Too often, leadership trainers focus on the process they are trying to create or the developmental experience for the leader. What we are suggesting is that you know the impact point you are trying to affect with the introduction of a leadership development intervention.

■ *View your investment in leadership development like any other business investment and estimate the return on development.* This ROD should be based on the performance impact point you are trying to achieve, the number of leaders you want to have at a certain level of competency, and the challenges and opportunities you are preparing them to address.

■ *Leadership is not inherent, even though some attributes that relate to leadership have some genetic input.* What we're finding is that one's genes predispose but do not preordain one to lead. There is a very significant interaction that occurs between genetic predispositions and the environment, and it helps shape human and leadership development over time.

■ *Trigger events may represent those incidents that are accelerants for authentic leadership development in organizations.* We find that brief moments in life seem to have a lasting positive impact on a leader's development, if the leader has taken the time to reflect and learn from those moments. Encouraging managers to think about the moments they want to create with followers is part of the authentic leadership development that occurs in organizations every day

4

MAPPING THE
JOURNEY OF ALD

ONE OF OUR MAIN goals in writing this book was to provide you a "visual map" for your ALD journey. To frame this journey in the right context, we felt it was important for you to visualize ALD as something very personal. This map incorporates a model or theory of yourself, and in more generalized terms, how you influence just one other person, on up to hundreds or even thousands of followers or peers. The exact number would depend on your constituency.

We need to stretch the idea of ALD from the inside to the outside right into the future. Then, as we have repeatedly said up to this point, you need to bring that future back into the present. Effective authentic leaders are able to bring their dreams, strategic vision, and values back to the present reality.

If we were presenting this as a treasure map, the beginning and ending point would in effect be the same point. This is where X marks the spot. For each cycle in the ALD process, it is fundamentally important that we begin and end with your self-awareness. However, your ending self-awareness will be enhanced by the experience of doing something consistently different. And when you get back to that X again, the routes on your map of ALD will change, since you can now take new directions and embark on new adventures.

Kevin Cashman, a consultant who wrote about authentic leadership several years ago, recalled one of his clients who basically followed the self-awareness map we are describing:

> At the early stages of Jack's career, his cognitive and intellectual skills helped him excel in many challenging, complex assignments. As his achievements advanced, Jack started to believe his own "press" and internalized the belief that he was the person who "made things happen." Gradually his relationships became strained, and he couldn't understand why. To help Jack break through his self-limiting view, we asked him to outline key events in his life over the past two weeks by focusing on the people who had made each event possible. It didn't take him long to recognize the web of interdependence that was supporting his success. He became aware of initiatives for which he had taken credit and for which he now needed to acknowledge others. He was beginning to genuinely bridge personal power with synergy power to enhance his contribution.

In this example, Jack eventually came full circle on his self-awareness map. His map was enhanced by his journey, which ended at the same spot, but with Jack now a more authentic and effective leader.

Our ALD map has four basic core components:

1. Self-awareness
2. Self-regulation
3. Self-development
4. A new level of ALD

We will go into all of these in the course of this and ensuing chapters. In this chapter we will focus on the core component, self-awareness.

SELF-AWARENESS

There are many layers to what is meant by self-awareness. It does not mean "either—or," but rather, is a matter of degree. It cuts across insights you have about your own qualities, expectations, values, personality, attitude, efficacy, behavior, and actions. Self-awareness also affects how these apply to your relationships with others in the past, present, and future. Let us offer some examples for you to reflect upon in order to assess your self-awareness:

- Do you know what your core organizing value in life is?
- Do you know what you don't know about your closest colleague?
- Do you know how you come across to the newest associate working with you?
- Do you know how you are perceived by associates of a different ethnic group than your own?
- How does the opposite sex perceive your leadership style?
- Have you thought about how you dealt with the most significant challenge you had with an associate recently and whether you could have approached that person differently at the outset?
- What is your number one strength, and how have you leveraged that strength in your work over the last six months?
- What do you think your least preferred coworker thinks about your leadership approach?
- Looking back over the past week, what is your approximate ratio of positive to negative comments?

- What is the most important insight you have gained from dealing with or traveling to another culture?
- Do you know what your top priority is for each week?
- What is your life priority above all else in relation to your work?
- In terms of your job, what do you fear most, and has that changed since you first started in this job? Where does that fear come from?

The above list of items is not exhaustive. In truth, the questions that link to anyone's self-awareness are nearly infinite. We can take almost any aspect of yourself, from values to behavior, and explore what you know, what you don't know, what you would like to know, and what you're afraid of knowing about yourself. Since there is so much you can question, we need to narrow it a bit. We need a plan to address the enhancement of your self-awareness so it contributes to your ALD.

However, we don't want you to randomly choose what you think will or will not impact your self-awareness for ALD. Since our goal is to accelerate your ALD, we're concerned with what aspect of your self-awareness will have the greatest potential leverage for your development as an authentic leader. To gain the greatest return on development (ROD), we'll begin by defining what we mean by self-awareness in terms of the past, present, and future, and on two levels: that of yourself and yourself with others.

Look Back Self-Awareness

The older we get, the more information we have to reflect on, if we choose to do so. This is because our base is so much larger and continues to grow over time. Of course, the interesting thing about reflecting back is that the same event may very well be perceived differently. This perception will depend on your experiences and your reflections since the last time you thought back about a particular moment in time. Has that ever happened to you? Have you had multiple reflections on the same event? Did these various reflections cause you to go deeper in your understanding of that event?

If you have not done so, then we need to be building discipline whose aim is to take time to look back in order to grow forward in your development. Some events should be reviewed again and again. These can be good stories about what happened, why it happened, what you learned, and how it changed what you did. Remembering our earlier example of the retail CEO's history class in college, even one well-known battle can be seen in three distinctly different ways.

To reiterate, in certain moments, and looking back with the benefit of time, we may now view a moment that was initially viewed as negative earlier as a positive trigger now, in our ALD. An extreme example is a woman executive who recently told us that cancer was the best thing that happened to her. She came to this strange conclusion after reflecting upon how it had changed her life. Her look back included getting a much better handle on what she could and would accomplish, given what she felt was a much more limited time frame. Before cancer, she realized she had never set a single major life priority. She had allowed life to set priorities for her, rather than setting them herself.

As we pointed out at the outset of this book with the example of having a heart attack, negative trigger moments can cause us to reposition our priorities. The cancer survivor above became determined to not only beat the dreaded disease, but to reconfigure her life. The top priority was something she would think about, and do something about, each and every day for the rest of her life.

Often, leaders look back at how they handled a particular interaction with someone and say to themselves, "I could have been more persuasive if I had only known." The deeper dive here is: If they had only known something better about themselves *and* about the other person, the quality or moment of that interaction may have been significantly enhanced.

On the other side of the coin, how often do leaders stumble through the same issue or problem again and again? They repeat their behavior because they are not aware of how they could have acted or thought differently. Indeed, we believe this is one explanation as to why some executives get on that slippery slope toward unethical practices. They do not realize that even small indiscretions are moving them downhill. The only way we can systematically act differently is to be aware that there is at least one alternative that was not part of our past awareness, an alternative we now know of and can choose in the future.

Some of the best learning cases for leadership development come from reflecting on one's own past successes and failures.

At this point, think about how often in the last week you have gone back to events that occurred to try to figure out what you'd done, how you did it, and what you could do differently. Now think about the last month: How much time did you allocate to thinking about the way you've done something with others? How could you have taken one aspect of the interaction to improve your relationship?

Consider the oft-mentioned measurement known as "Six Sigma," which describes quantitatively how a process is performing. (To achieve Six Sigma, a process must not produce more than 3.4 defects per million opportunities.) Why is it that we are so thrilled with, and so willing to endorse operations in organizations involving "lean thinking" and "lean management" to improve to Six Sigma quality, yet we don't even think or do anything about variations in human behavior? This is especially true of our own behavior. We do not figure out how we might improve to a higher level of consistent quality interactions with others.

Imagine if each of your fellow leaders in your organization were to try to improve just one aspect of one interaction every week. Although this does not sound like a lot, in an organization like the one we are working with, which has 15,000 managers, it could be 15,000 improvements per week times 50 weeks, or 750,000 improvements in relationships over the year. More modestly, say you only hit on improving interactions half the time in this same company. Still, that would amount to 375,000 improved relationships. Just imagine how such self-awareness, in and of itself, could drive climate and cultural change in your organization. Think about the improvement in the social capital structure of your organization. In other words, consider how the network of relationships could transfer needed knowledge to those who required it in order to effectively perform the task and have an impact.

When we set out to discuss organizational transformation, regardless of the target, we invariably have to deal with each individual's level of self-awareness as a starting point. Yet in most cases, we hear the workforce was not aware of the magnitude of change that confronted them with a new initiative. It always starts with self-awareness. Later on, we need to understand the importance of the collective self-awareness that is gained when all people are firing in the same direction around a particular initiative.

Present Self-Awareness

These days, it has become tricky to talk about the present. This is because the time boundaries around the present may be only moments or days, not even weeks, in some people's perception. For our purposes, let's say that the present is what is happening this week in one's life.

To build self-awareness in this present state, one needs a plan or framework to activate conscious attention to what is transpiring around you. You might say that you're trying to "prime" yourself to focus on aspects of the way you think, feel, and behave. You need this plan to be cognizant of who you are, and the impact you have, when you interact with others.

The plan can be as simple as going into your meetings knowing the ratio you try to maintain of positive to negative comments. A method that effective executive coaches often use is to have their clients focus on such straightforward plans in order to make them aware of how they come across to others. Ideally, the process we're creating here is in effect a self-driven or self-coaching model, which hopefully is based on an ALD approach.

What do we mean by authentic in this case? It means it is based on what we know and have learned. The intervention—for instance, your ratio of positive over negative comments—can have the intended positive impact on your ALD.

You need a very simple plan to help trigger self-awareness each day.

This recommendation for your ALD is based on some very sophisticated research conducted by positive psychologists Barbara Frederickson and colleagues at the University of Michigan. Briefly, the research involved videotaping 60 top management teams interacting at the Michigan executive training center. After completion of the program, the researchers coded the videotaped recordings for the number of positive and negative comments uttered during these sessions. What they found was intriguing.

Essentially, those teams that maintained a ratio of 2.911 positive comments to negative ones had interactions that were rated more effective and were based on inquiry versus advocacy. The executive groups in the inquiry mode went deeper into analyzing problems, challenges, and issues, as opposed to simply advocating a position and taking "their" stand to the exclusion of all others.

The practical lesson from this research is that to lead a group that is digging deeper into issues, rather than simply presenting a position, it is recommended to err in the direction of being more positive than negative. Why? Negative information almost always carries more weight in a conversation, and therefore to counterbalance these inevitable negatives requires proportionately (the research says about three-to-one) more positive comments.

So now, think back to your last several meetings. Did your group spend more time in advocacy or inquiry mode? What do you think the ratio of positive to negative comments was in your group's interactions? If you want more inquiry that better probes the problems and issues, the positive interactions and comments should be about three-to-one over the negative ones.

THE ROLE OF SELF-EFFICACY

Let's take a look at something else in the present that might help your self-awareness and the way you interact with others. A colleague of ours said recently that every time you meet someone who is either new or familiar, you either build trust or you subtract from trust. This zero-sum game is an easy thing to remember, so let's apply it to some other psychological capacity, such as developing self-efficacy.

Self-efficacy refers to the probability you have in mind—your confidence—that you will be successful in taking on a particular task or challenge. Through an extensive meta-analysis (114 studies) conducted by Fred and Alex Stajkovic, self-efficacy was found to improve work-related performance on average by an impressive 28 percent.

We believe a central role of ALD is to build up not only your own self-efficacy, or confidence, for improved performance, but that of others as well. Indeed, a by-product of one's ALD involves developing leadership in followers through enhancing their self-efficacy to lead others. In other words, ALD has a trickle down or cascading effect through the mechanism of self-efficacy.

As you enter into an interaction or conversation about a particular task with an associate, how do you describe the goals, resources, challenges, and potential obstacles for achieving that task? What do you do to build their self-efficacy? Do you emphasize their successes in the past on similar projects?

Do you emphasize your availability to make sure they succeed? Do you emphasize the quality of the support or equipment/technology they have to do their job? Do you provide positive feedback when they show signs of progress? All of these in each interaction have been shown through research findings to potentially add to their level of self-efficacy.

Again drawing from a substantial research base, the antecedents to enhancing self-efficacy are very clear. Specifically, the questions we posed above point to ways this occurs with real challenges and projects. Put simply, how can you increase, even by 10 percent, for example, the probability that associates believe they can improve their chances of being successful? Do you think it is about their confidence in their ability to take on the challenge? Do you think it is about their view of the equipment and technology they have to be successful?

Recent research relevant to this last question has found that "means efficacy" is important when it comes to how successful people think they will be in a job. What this means is that they feel they have the right tools, even the best tools, to do the job. This "means efficacy" has been found to have a strong impact on effective performance.

How about your own self-efficacy for taking on a challenge? Have you entered into situations where the script in your head is "can't versus can"?

A significant part of effective sports psychology involves training world-class athletes to "visualize" success. Bruce recalls walking into a learning lab at West Point where a group of football players were glued to a highlights video showing incredible bone-crunching tackles. Bang! Bang! Cheers and growls from the observers. The coaches wanted to get in their players' heads what an absolutely perfect hit looked like. They were trying to get them to visualize it so that on the field they could draw confidence from successful tackling, without actually experiencing it themselves.

Such modeling of successful behavior has been demonstrated to have a powerful impact on building self-efficacy. For example, Fred plays a lot of golf. His scores are usually in the high 80s or low 90s, and his golfing buddies regularly beat him. Yet, for some reason, he still thinks he's pretty good and that he should beat them. He still has a lot of confidence in his game and constantly believes that his breakout will occur in his next outing. In other words, his self-efficacy for golf is quite high. But in contrast to the theory and research—and much to his chagrin—he has not directly experienced success, by any rational metric.

Upon careful self-analysis of this quandary, Fred recently reflected back to where this golf efficacy could have come from. Like many other moments that matter, he traced it back to when he was a youngster in the 1950s. Fred and his friends caddied (it was a lot like the movie *Caddy Shack*). It happened that the young man he regularly caddied for went on to win the Iowa Amateur. Fred remembered watching this successful golfer up close and personal and saying to himself, "I can do that."

Fred thinks that these moments of observing and modeling this excellent golfer's success those many years ago has carried over to affect his present golf efficacy. He doesn't get the same effect from watching a Tiger Woods or even a Jack Nicklaus, who is more in his age range, because they are not relevant role models for him. But that young guy whom he caddied for, and whom he knew quite well and could relate to, has been an abiding influence on his self-efficacy, though he has not directly experienced that same golfing success.

Do you have a similar story that may help explain the inexplicable efficacy (high or low) you may have in some aspect of your leadership?

Have you ever met someone who said something like, "I just seem to be able to get people to move in the right direction, and have always been able to, since I was a kid." What we and others have found is that early leadership experiences taught these people what worked and what didn't work concerning leadership.

Often, people can describe a particular leadership moment during which, by taking a stand or charting a course, they were able to be successful as a leader. We now know that such previous leadership moments can have a profoundly positive impact on a leader's level of self-efficacy to lead, or what some colleagues of ours have called "motivation to lead."

THE ROLE OF SELF-FULFILLING PROPHECY

Think about situations in which you're hesitant to take the lead, and your "self-talk" is about what you are not likely to be successful at doing. Such negative arguments are based on a fundamental motivational principle called "self-fulfilling prophecy." You think negatively, and so it happens that you do indeed have negative results.

By the way, the studies from the meta-analysis of 100 years of research on leadership development presented in the last chapter showed that one of the greatest impacts was based on this principle; what we called the "Pygmalion Effect." Of course, with this powerful self-fulfilling prophecy proving itself, you fail miserably again and again, which in turn negatively affects your self-efficacy.

But this self-fulfilling prophecy can work in a positive direction as well. The fact is, most people tend to underestimate what their upward potential is in most performance domains. To get people tracking in a positive prophecy, they need to begin building self-efficacy in order to stretch into that high performance domain through, for instance, positive visualization and self-talk. Not only does this potentially positively impact your own likelihood of success, it can also improve the self-efficacy and success of those around you.

The so-called trickle-down, cascading, or contagion effect, as we said earlier, is based on modeling (remember Fred's golf game). What you say to yourself certainly impacts your self-efficacy, but also, how you demonstrate your beliefs in yourself will cascade either positively or negatively, affecting how others believe in you and themselves. This is the power of self-awareness that ultimately, over time, can be observed in the "collective efficacy" of your followers. Just like self-efficacy, there is considerable research evidence that this collective efficacy has a strong positive impact on performance.

Future Self-Awareness

To some degree, future self-awareness is a lot like the present, except, of course, you have to dig down and probe further out into the future than you do in the present. However, in addition to a future orientation, we know that one way to be more self-aware about the future is to be keenly aware of what can be called the "emerging present."

In an increasing number of industries, cycle times for how long it takes for a new innovation to become a standard product, and then in turn to become obsolete, is very short these days. As a result, the emerging present has become more obvious. Bruce recalls a conversation with a former adult student who had worked at Intel and noted that long-term planning was usually stretched out to 18 to 24 months. Indeed, Andy Grove, former chairman of Intel, came up with the concept of "zero segment time." What he meant was how long it took the most innovative product to become something you'd throw away as no longer useful to any market segment. And the time band in which this occurs has shrunk, and continues to shrink.

At Japanese-based companies such as Toyota and Pioneer Electronics, long-term planning is considered to be five to seven years. However, there are some distinct cultural influences affecting this. In Asian cultures, managers have a longer-term perspective than managers in Western cultures. This cultural difference also affects the "thinking out" time frame of individuals within the culture. Asians in collectivistic and Confucian-oriented cultures tend to think further out, and to reinforce such thinking in their leaders.

In highly individualistic cultures, as in the United States, such "way out" thinking is often scoffed at as being too "blue sky" or unrealistic and too academic or idealistic. Americans feel that a future orientation is necessary and draw from research in advocating the importance of a future orientation.

Across all cultures, but in some more than others, there is a necessary discipline in order to remain cognizant of emerging trends in parallel fields that might affect your business: what you do in your job role, and what you do with others. Go back 10 or 15 years. Would you ever have imagined that much of the work that is now being done every day is with people you never meet with face-to-face? Back then, virtual work was in its infancy and thought to be futuristic fantasy.

As the world became connected, it would have been helpful to begin speculating about how this interconnectedness would impact not only work, but also leadership, relationships with others, networks of contacts, business-to-business models, work stress, and outsourcing. Also, speculation on the impact of the Internet on banking, shopping, traveling, education, medicine, and so on would have been wise. There is a reason why some expert observers have called the Internet a disruptive technology, or more positively, a transforming technology.

The ALD process builds self-efficacy in the future by pulling leaders' futures into the present. This is accomplished by identifying emerging trends that may shape what the future will look like to them. They discipline themselves to read and explore at the boundaries, beyond their expertise and interests. They build a constituency and network to keep them informed about new developments that might affect the core aspects of what makes them successful. Indeed, if you only stay informed on what your domain currently produces, you're probably not aware of significant emerging trends that will impact on your future from other domains of knowledge.

For example, if you are in consumer products and retailing, are you on top of the newly emerging RFID (radio frequency identification) technology? Wal-Mart operations managers are demanding that its top 100 suppliers have this new technology in place (small electronic tags affixed to products for tracking purposes) in order to reduce distribution time and costs.

Another example is the Starbucks coffee king, Howard Schultz. In the words of *Fast Company*, Schultz is "thinking outside the cup" these days. Far from coffee, he is making moves to put Starbucks into the music business (individual music-listening stations, with CD-burning capabilities, in their existing coffeehouses). "Great companies," he's said, "are defined by their discipline and their understanding of who they are and who they are not. But also, great companies must have the courage to examine strategic opportunities that are transformational—as long as they are not inconsistent with the guiding principles and values of the core business." His comments mirror what we are advocating when we talk about bringing self-awareness of the future back to the present.

Although you may not come up with *the* grand idea as Howard Schultz did, you can come to the realization that the future can be created in small increments. Over time, these increments may explode into an unbelievable significant trend. Yet few, if any, breakthroughs show up on the scene unannounced. In truth, every great innovation or transformative change lingered in the minds and actions of many people before the noticeable change occurred. This is true in both the social and natural sciences.

Ideas have often arisen from seemingly insignificant things. An example would be the simple stent. This little piece of metal that resembles a spring for a ballpoint pen generated a whopping $4.5 billion in revenue in 2004 and made more profits than a blockbuster drug. Stents are now commonly used to open clogged arteries (we seem to be on this heart disease theme for leadership development). In another example, kids were commonly instant messaging each other long before the business community ever heard of the Blackberry device!

If you read about some breakthrough, it is probably too late. You need to get out of your usual routines, spend a day with some protest movement, go to a bar where there are only young people, observe what kids in college think is "awesome," and/or spend some time on the firing line with your troops. Such firsthand information may serve as triggers to bring the future back to the present.

The future is always emerging in the present for the highly self-aware leader.

FOR YOU TO DO ON YOUR ALD JOURNEY

Think about how your leader creates the conditions for self-awareness around priority issues. For example, the CEO of JetBlue, David Neelman, runs an internal program on leadership called, "Principles of Leadership," and on the first day he asks, "Why are you here?"

What similar examples can you come up with in your own domain of interest? We bet there are many. To help build your own self-awareness into the future for ALD, think about the following questions or requests and jot down answers in your journal:

1. Do you have people around you who introduce ideas from other domains totally unfamiliar to you?
2. Look back over the last year and categorize what you have read or had conversations about in your familiar domain and unfamiliar domain. What is the balance of reading and talking you do in and outside your domain? What is the balance you would like to (should) have?
3. Do you ever attend seminars that have nothing directly to do with your discipline or domain of work?
4. Think out 25 years. What will health care (or retailing or manufacturing) be like in 25 years? How will you learn? What jobs will be extinct? What will be on the History channel that is now a hot commodity? What will constitute an organization? How will you travel? What will be used for money? How will leaders be developed?
5. Take a look at your newest associate. After working a year with this individual, what would be the most important contribution you would like to make in his or her development? What pathways would you have built to accomplish that objective?
6. Take a look at what you want to learn that would change your capacity to lead in a particular area. For example, if you want to improve the impact you have via presentations, then try and think about what you can do to be a more effective presenter in the future.
7. Try to imagine 100 years out what family, education, work, technology, and travel might look like. Now go 150 years out; 200 years. How far can you imagine into the future what life would be like? Can you learn anything for use in the present?
8. If you have children (now or later), accelerate them into the future. They are having a conversation with a best friend and describing the one core value that you drilled into them as

being singularly most important to their development. What value would you choose and how would you assure that it is the one your child relays to his or her friend in that moment that matters?

LEADERSHIP NOTES

- *The root of leadership development is in self-awareness.* To become more self-aware, one must realize that the present, like the future, is emerging. You need to examine how you engage the present and why it will give you some insights into what the future holds. Self-awareness is best learned by focusing on just one area at a time. For example: How positive am I each morning and why?

- *Like any form of development, one needs a plan.* To move forward in leadership development, we have found that the greatest positive gains occur for those individuals who have a specific goal and plan and are able to identify the support needed to accomplish that goal.

- *At the base of effective leadership is what we call self-efficacy, or confidence.* The idea of self-efficacy represents your inner confidence about your ability to accomplish a specific challenge, such as: What's the probability that you believe you can develop the best talents of your followers into strengths?

5

ACTUAL SELF TO POSSIBLE SELF EQUALS AUTHENTIC SELF

HAVE YOU EVER SAID or heard someone else say, "I was at my best when . . . "? This observation is commonly heard from star athletes being interviewed, but it applies equally well to other domains: in education, social and family relations, and the workplace. The point is that we all serve in many different roles in life, and indeed throughout each and every day.

We all have multiple roles, and these many "selves" collectively constitute what is commonly referred to as one's self-image. For example, we can view our "selves" as a child, parent, friend, neighbor, man or woman, coworker, mentor, or leader.

In each sphere of life, we can describe ourselves as what we actually are, or what we possibly want to become over time. This can be referred to as our "actual self" and our "possible self." We all carry in our head this important dynamic balance between our actual self and our possible self. The same is true of the followers of leaders.

An important component of ALD for both leaders and their followers is to move the actual self to what is possible. For example, both leaders and followers may not view their actual selves as being effective communicators with large groups. However, over time, with coaching and sufficient support, we may become effective with large groups, and this great communicator then becomes who we are. In other words, our possible self has become our actual self, or what we would call our authentic self.

There is no such thing as a single "self."

MOVING FROM ACTUAL TO POSSIBLE

To dig deeper into this part of the ALD process, we ask you to ponder the following question: How many people really fully understand what constitutes being a parent before that first child is actually born? Now, moving forward 15 years after your child is born, it is probably difficult for a parent to imagine a time where being a parent was not part of their self-image.

Some selves should and do change over time, as challenges in our lives change. As Paul Wieand of the Center for Advanced Emotional Intelligence notes: "In a time when change is the only constant, a leader's self-concept can't remain fixed." However, ALD is also about changing the cycle of life's development, to move from the actual to the possible self in a more efficient manner.

Let's use some simple examples to contrast these two forms of self:

Role	Actual Self	Possible Self
1. Parent	Focus on what child does wrong.	Take time each day to reinforce positives.
2. Friend	Hesitant to ask for help.	Seek out opinions on important matters.
3. Coworker	Contribute based on what I get in return.	Find opportunities to sacrifice for others.
4. Leader	Stickler about bureaucratic rules as an end.	Reinforce breaking bureaucratic rules as an end for speed and creativity.

In essence, development, whether traditional, personal, or ALD, is all about going from what we (and others) perceive as our actual to our possible self. It is trying to close this gap, or at least narrow it, that makes ALD challenging. And, of course, the wider the gap that needs to be changed in the individual, the greater the challenge.

Parents, spouses, or significant others in the personal realm, and mentors and coaches in the leadership domain, often see and can better identify the gap between actual and possible before the individual does. Frequently, commenting on their coach, we have heard leaders say about their potential: "They were able to see in me something I did not yet recognize in myself."

Many leaders do not even consider their possible self because they have become too comfortable with their actual self. As AEI's Wieand observes in many of his top level clients, "You start playing a role that the corporate culture and the general culture expect you to play. And suddenly you're thinking that you've got it all figured out, when all you've got is hubris."

Leadership developers may see something in us that we didn't see in ourselves.

An important part of ALD involves someone seeing in you the actual-possible gap, and then orchestrating the conditions to narrow this discrepancy over time. This bridging between actual and possible takes place even if you are not initially fully prepared to do so. How can others help you do this, and how can you do it for yourself and with others? Let's start with how others can do it with you.

HOW OTHERS CAN FACILITATE YOUR ACTUAL TO POSSIBLE SELF

Many times, your parents, best friends, coach, or mentor has successfully lived through the challenges you are currently confronting. They may already be living in their and your "possible."

Life has its cycles, and those ahead in the cycle can look back and provide you with insights and lessons that they see could be valuable to accelerating your development. It may be a point they have crossed in their lives, and they know the bridge that is necessary for you to take to avoid some of the pitfalls they were unable to avoid in their own development cycle.

Others may be operating in your future before you are. But you must be able to listen to them and empathize; to see the relevance. Often, however, we are not prepared to do so.

This does not mean you don't hear others ahead of you. It means you cannot translate their message into something relevant and meaningful for your own ALD. Indeed, this is true in many instances, whether it's operating in the role of a parent, friend, teacher, coach, mentor, or leader. The challenge for them is to convince you they have "been there and done that," even if "that" is a bit different from what you are directly experiencing and confronting.

Part of being a great coach is the ability to translate experienced events into meaningful learning for those who have not yet experienced these challenges. The message of the coach, friend, or whomever has to be literally translated so it applies to what the learner can understand and apply to him- or herself.

An example would be the great warrior Crazy Horse. After he led the Sioux to victory over Custer, his friend and confidant He Dog strongly opposed Crazy Horse's continued forays against the miners who were invading the Black Hills with gold fever. In the 1930s, while being interviewed by Eleanor Hinman, a Nebraska schoolteacher, the then 90-something He Dog told her he said to Crazy Horse: "My friend, you are past the foolish years of the wild young warrior; you belong to the people now and must think of them, not give them such uneasiness."

Obviously, Crazy Horse did not heed this message, nor the one He Dog gave him when he decided to negotiate a truce: "Look out—watch your step—you are going into a dangerous place". On this mission, Crazy Horse ended up being escorted to the infamous Fort Robinson, Nebraska, guard house where, after a scuffle, he was stabbed and killed. One moral of this tragic ending of a great leader is that others close to the leader need to provide relevant stories or messages that are believed by the learner; this is a good place to begin in terms of developing others.

Leaders or followers being developed may not have directly lived or experienced the possible self, but still may have observed it occurring with others. We can learn from others who have successfully met the challenges we now confront, and that the others are then able to share with you, telling you how they did it. All this assumes that one is willing to listen hard and believe what he or she is told.

Sometimes the others were not necessarily successful themselves with the challenge you are now confronting. However, they have come to realize over time what it takes to be successful, so they can now share this experience with you.

The beauty of a parent, coach, mentor, or friend is that they can take a negative moment for them and turn it into a positive moment for your ALD. It can serve as a catalyst and make your leadership development far less painful.

OTHERS CAN BREAK YOU OUT OF YOUR AUTOMATIC PROCESSING

Effective mentors or coaches for ALD take the time to carefully observe and monitor how we engage our relationships, work, and challenges. They can see where you may come up short, not necessarily based on ability, but because they have experienced the challenge themselves, or have seen others with less ability take on the challenge successfully. If ability is not a factor, they may conclude that you may be making a choice not to succeed, either consciously or unconsciously.

Every day we make hundreds if not thousands of choices. Unfortunately, we are not always aware whether we are optimizing our full potential, our possible selves, in even a small percentage of those moments. A key is to take advantage of those moments that matter when they arise unplanned.

Have you ever had someone give you feedback on how you went over in a large group setting in which you did not feel you connected? Were you at ease with their feedback? Did you listen hard to what they had to say?

We all develop patterns of interactions that become almost automatic, when our responses come out without much thought behind them. By the way, responding in such an automatic way can also be a good thing, since we cannot always stop to carefully process everything. We develop ways to short-circuit deep processing to get through decisions that are not consequential, which is the main premise for Malcolm Gladwell's new book, *Blink*.

What happens over time is that we build these automatic or "packaged responses" to move from decision point to decision point more efficiently. What our coaches or mentors can do for us is help us "unpackage" some of these automatic responses. They can help us look at our automatics with more controlled attention to see whether an alternative response is more appropriate.

In essence, significant others can slow us down when it comes to processing and deciding, which can help us reconfigure how we might best approach situations. In the past we may have felt an automatic response was sufficient.

This difference between automatic and controlled processing can be seen in how General George Patton approached things as compared to General Eisenhower. Historian Stephen Ambrose observed that "Patton was an erratic genius capable of sustained action but not systematic thought. Eisenhower had a steady, orderly mind. When he looked at a problem, he would take everything into account, weigh possible alternatives, and deliberately decide on a course of action."

Although starting off as junior to Patton, when Eisenhower became his boss, he tried to mentor and guide Patton's unbridled, automatic thought processes. Unfortunately, Eisenhower's attempt at moving Patton to his possible self did not bear fruit. Although a hero in the War, Patton ended his career as, at best, a tarnished leader because he did not seem capable of moving to his possible self.

THE SELF-DISCIPLINE TO MOVE TO YOUR POSSIBLE SELF

Besides the important role others can play, your ALD to achieve possible self also requires self-discipline. For instance, think back to when you entered into a heated conversation: What was your breathing pattern like? If you can control your breathing, you can control the oxygen going to your brain. Research has shown that this oxygen supply fuels better dialogue. Perhaps you can apply this one simple rule to improve your self-discipline.

Another rule for self-disciplining yourself might be something like: Never send an e-mail when your heart rate is pumping 20 beats above its normal resting pace. Or, at the beginning of every meeting with your staff, highlight what was accomplished since the last meeting and thank those involved before beginning your agenda.

One of leadership consultant Paul Wieand's clients at AEI, for example, now "begins each meeting by speaking candidly—and, at times emotionally—about what he has been dealing with in the bank that week. And he's found that his candor has sparked true dialogue." This bank leader has moved to his possible, open, and more authentic self by this simple rule of how he starts a meeting with his staff.

Another young IT manager has taken the moments idea and used it in starting off every week with what he calls "Monday moments." He covers the last week's moments and the positive and challenging ones on the horizon. The meeting is scheduled for only 15 minutes for high, positive impact.

In an interview on the A&E biography channel, Oprah Winfrey was asked why so many people connected to her from so many different walks of life. Her intriguing response was that she always revealed things about herself that others would prefer to keep behind the scenes.

Oprah has put herself out there, making herself vulnerable about her weight problems, dealing with race relations, and her fears. By doing so, she worked out her actual self in front of America, and moved to what was possible for herself to accomplish in her career and in her life. She had the self-confidence to make herself vulnerable to learn from herself and others.

LEADING ASSOCIATES TO THEIR POSSIBLE SELVES

Finally, in addition to listening to others and gaining self-discipline, in your ALD you must also coach and facilitate associates to attain their possible selves. For example, when meeting new people with whom you will be working, try to explore what is their actual selves.

The key is to get to something your associates would most like to accomplish. Specifically, try to get to what they think they are best at doing. This will help with finding the right fit in your selection process, and over time facilitate their development. That way, they will be able to build from strength versus "focus first on weakness."

What about your current associates? Do you know what they think they do best? Are they currently doing it? Do you have this knowledge for every employee who works directly or indirectly with you? Do you know what type of recognition the people who work with you like to receive? Do your people know what kind of recognition is most important to you?

Building off your self-discipline, as discussed above, the answers to these questions can be translated into simple rules to help you go from your automatic to your controlled processing mode. These rules can help you stop and think about how you impact yourself and others.

The longer we know someone, the more likely it is that we automatically process information about them. Unfortunately, this automaticity may cause us to miss something significant. Anyone who has had a long-term relationship knows exactly what we are referring to here.

To be socially adept, we have to operate using certain assumptions that guide how rapidly we process information. And likely, it will be very difficult to slow down or prevent automatic processing. Yet, in your ALD, we advocate going back through self-reflection to explore and then question your base assumptions, to make sure they are still appropriate.

You have to follow some of the basic rules we have suggested above to help yourself and others move from their actual to their possible selves. Since we can slow it down in most instances, we suggest circling back and taking another look at the situation that you confronted. Indeed, with great moments in life, people circle back endlessly, learning a little more each time they return to a significant event about themselves.

The challenge now in front of you is to try and identify your actual selves in terms of the different roles you partake in through work and outside of work. Some people are much better at first looking into themselves and then others because of the training, coaching, counseling, mentoring, or even the great parenting they received. Nevertheless, within the normal range of human behavior, we can all improve in this regard.

The improvements will first be reflected in the self-discipline you show in taking on the task of your own ALD. This not only moves you to what's possible, it also moves others through your role modeling. In this way they can also choose to develop their own possible selves.

Self-discipline around aspects of our actual self help provide the basis for what is possible in terms of one's development.

LEARNING FROM OTHERS

There are two powerful forms of learning from others. These social learning processes typically require little conscious effort and have a long history of effectiveness.

The first is called "vicarious learning." This is learning that occurs through direct observation of others' actions that are being reinforced. When you go into a situation or an organization in which you have no experience, you learn a lot through vicarious observation.

An example of vicarious learning would be when we first went to work with the Gallup Organization as senior scientists. It quickly became clear to us, by observing interactions and through numerous conversations, that "Gallupers" frequently refer to what they have done or accomplished based on leveraging their strengths. For instance, toward the end of one of the first meetings Bruce had at Gallup one of the participants said, "Let me take the lead on coordinating that because I am high on 'arranger.'"

Each Gallup employee and most of their clients know by heart their top five strengths. They find these out through the well-known Clifton StrengthsFinder Profile. You can also take this instrument to find your own top five strengths by going to the Gallup Web site (http://www.Gallup.com). For our purposes, these identified strengths can be discussed and leveraged vicariously each and every day.

Given how fast people process information, vicarious learning can be a very powerful approach and specific technique for ALD. Since you are watching others almost all the time, and others are also watching you, the quality and authenticity of this observed behavior may be a much more powerful ALD program than going away for an expensive leadership development program at a hotel.

The second form of social learning, closely related to vicarious learning, is called "role modeling." Not everyone is created equal when it comes to role modeling. Leaders in organizations, by definition or default, represent some sort of success. Consequently, followers will mirror the behavior of their organizational leaders because they believe that such behavior defines what is successful, given the leaders' position and accomplishments.

As an example of role modeling, we can see how our children dress, speak, and act toward each other in a given period of time. Often we can connect this strange behavior to someone famous, like Britney Spears or Justin Timberlake, at least when they were "in" (we'll have to ask our children who's in now, or grandchildren, in Fred's case). The kids are simply modeling the celebrity's behavior.

The point is, the language, nuances, and patterns of behavior we observe in teenagers, employees, citizens of other countries, and ourselves are often rooted in the behavior we identify as relevant role models. Indeed, such role models are so powerful in terms of the impact on our learning, that their impact on our behavior almost becomes automatic. In other words, the observed behavior/actions of our role models become incorporated into our own ways of behaving. This is because we see them as being associated with success, or at least something that is desirable.

With both vicarious learning and role modeling, we can conclude that leaders basically set the conditions or tone for our actions and behavior. Consider, for instance, an article that appeared in the *New York Times* on August 19, 2004: "Abuse Inquiry Faults Officers on Leadership." In the first line, the reporter states: "A high level Army inquiry has found that senior American commanders created the conditions that allowed abuses to occur at Abu Ghraib prison in Iraq . . ." The important words in this article's opening line for us are "created the conditions."

Leaders create the conditions by what they say, what they don't say, how they say it, what they follow up and do or don't do. These conditions determine what leaders reinforce and what they ignore or punish. Leaders stand out and are therefore closely watched to see what signals they offer for directing the behavior and decisions of their followers.

An example of the importance of setting the conditions is provided by well-known marketing professor Len Berry. Conducting an intensive, long-term study of the famed Mayo Clinic, he found numerous instances where leaders created supporting conditions for their followers. As one Mayo internist relayed to Berry: "The strong collegial attitude at Mayo allows me to call any Mayo physician at any time and discuss a patient in a tactful and pleasant manner. I do not feel afraid or stupid when I call a world-renowned Mayo surgeon. We respect each other. We help each other. We learn from each other." Is it any wonder that the clinic has become the health care institution of choice in the world, and last year served more than half a million patients and had over $4 billion in revenue?

A staff assistant at a prestigious university is at a picnic having a conversation with her husband and a renowned tenured professor:

> I huddle over beans and potato salad between husband and
> full-fledged tenured professor . . . I am not a Ph.D.-seeking

peer, nor faculty peer, nor even presume the respectability of spouse to such as these. I am departmental support, open understanding ear, pencil provider, and scribble reader rolled into only me. I spend time talking with the tenured professor on my left. So personable, he happily shares his summer vacation, his wife, his daughters, as meticulously my paper plate becomes visible. The conversation turns from family to accomplishment and worth. I listen intently as the subject line takes a bead upon me. The professor turns his head, seriousness in his manner and eye, and states, "Never underestimate your value." Me valuable? Until that very moment I had never considered myself in terms of value.

In this moment, a specific reinforcing question from a well-respected individual can be one of those moments that matter.

Bruce recently received an e-mail from a former undergraduate student who had been seriously injured playing soccer while taking his introductory leadership class. She indicated, when she first came to class after her injury, that Bruce had said, "Don't worry, whatever time it takes, you are going to master this leadership stuff." She was e-mailing him to say it had taken her over a decade, but she was almost done mastering the work on leadership required to complete her doctorate.

Like the Mayo doctor, staff assistant, or student examples above, all of us must interpret what leaders have said or not said. However, even more important than the words are the observed actions and behaviors. As Native American tribal leaders were known to say in their dealings with the territorial government and military leaders in the late 1800s, "Your actions speak so loud that we can no longer hear your words."

When asked to recall a moment in her life that affected her leadership development, a college student had the following to say: "I worked with a leader who consistently was inconsistent with the people around him. He would establish expectations and goals, but never follow through on them. Over time, I have thought about this leader in instances where I knew I did not want to be that type of leader."

Another student indicated that all of his closest friends in eighth grade got heavily involved with drugs and alcohol. For a while these friends didn't give him much grief for failing to fully participate with them at parties. However, eventually the peer pressure became so great that he had to make a conscious decision whether to stay with his friends and conform, or to attempt to build a new set of friends. He chose the latter, but with lots of pain and anguish. For a long time he had no friends, but eventually he was able to build a network of new friendships among people who respected his choice. He has looked back on this moment many times over the last few years and now realizes that there are times in his life that he must take the stand that is right for him, and no one else. This is true for him regardless of what others think or the severe social penalties it may entail.

The trials and tribulations facing today's teens is not that far removed from today's organizational participants. What we all witness in every organizational scandal is someone in a position of power— a Dennis Kozlowski, Ken Lay, or Al Dunlap—who created the conditions for abuse to occur. This is true whether it is in a detention center holding prisoners of war or in a financial firm on Wall Street.

Leaders have to exercise self-discipline in terms of conveying to others their "line in the sand" or "red lines" of what is acceptable and unacceptable behavior. This requires constant attention on the leader's part to openly, as well as behind closed doors, set the boundaries. Unlike the coed's leader cited above, authentic leaders know that their behavior is always being monitored for consistency to the standards they have set. These leaders act accordingly to reinforce those standards every day.

Jane Smith of Spelman College recently was a keynote speaker at the inaugural gathering of our Gallup Leadership Institute Summit in Omaha, Nebraska. Jane's father was a minister, and a close friend of Martin Luther King's father, who was also a minister. On the very day that a church bombing precipitated the Birmingham riots, she was at a gathering in her parents' living room with Dr. King when he first heard what happened. She recalled for us what she had observed as a young girl.

Dr. King, clearly shaken, went to the privacy of a bedroom and summoned a diversity of opinions—from a Jew, a white person, an elderly person, a woman, and a close male confidant, more or less in that order. This moment symbolized for her Dr. King's constant attention to getting a diverse input from everyone and building a broad coalition of supporters, regardless of race, religion, age, or gender. It was in that significant moment of vicarious learning that Dr. King's views of diversity came shining through to Jane Smith—and to the thousands like us, who were greatly affected by her telling this story through the years. Moments matter.

As we all walk through life, we come across such consistencies as shown by Dr. King in our leaders' behavior. These observed moments strongly cement in our minds what our leaders' value and what they don't. Once you are in a leadership role, you are on stage, and totally open and exposed to being judged. You are constantly teaching what is important to you, whether you're aware of it or not. It is through your consistency in words, deeds, and actions that you help others learn your values.

Leaders are constantly watched for what others believe is the right thing to do.

Leadership requires you to operate with sort of a split screen, at least in the beginning. Keep in mind that your actions impact not only what gets done, but what is thought about in terms of what gets done, and what could be done. Your behavior signals others what they need to do, what is important, and what can help them to be successful like you. It's easy to see the importance of how you behave. However, unfortunately, people also learn vicariously through poor role models, inauthentic leaders.

Have you ever been in a situation where the leader says one thing but acts differently? Some people were surprised, to say the least, to hear the tapes of President Nixon's conversations in the Oval Office, when he used profanity and racial slurs in conversations with the Reverend Billy Graham.

Reverend Graham has been the most respected individual in America since Gallup began taking such a poll many years ago. Given his impeccable character and observed tireless work with disenfranchised groups, many were shocked to hear of the inconsistency between his public and private messages. However, to his credit, and helping to restore his authenticity, Graham did appropriately apologize for this indiscretion. The apology helped him to remain one of our most respected leaders. Like one of the questions in our authentic leadership poll covered in Chapter 2, "He admitted when he made a mistake."

Leaders can certainly change their views and how they express them. However, as brought out in the Billy Graham example, the problem we have is when they change their public persona in private, and when they do so consistently. This breeds distrust and a following that is always second-guessing and spinning what the leader said.

You know you are in a relatively healthy organization when the leader takes a stand on some important issue, and everyone you talk to actually believes that is the leader's position without any question or spin. In other words, authentic leaders set the conditions for trust. As part of your ALD, you must learn to set such conditions and be consistent publicly and privately.

NOW, MAKING IT STICK

The most prevalent comment we hear from those returning from leadership training that they evaluated as being a very positive experience is that although the training was great, there was still a problem. The common complaint is that after the training, one returns to the normal grind (substitute here automatic thinking). They say, for instance, "I just reverted back to my old habits" (substitute automatic thinking again).

We question organizations and their leaders that continue to send people to training that is inconsistent with what they will support when those newly trained individuals return to the organization. We suspect that they believe such training moments can be the spark for significant change, but what they fail to realize is that no leadership trainer in the world can more powerfully move individuals than leaders who model the desired core value every day in their organizations. (Recall earlier that we asked you what your core value was. Now you need to consider how you deliver on that core value every day, and we mean *value* not *values*).

Both a great trainer and a great leader, who separately know the power of vicarious learning and role modeling, can in combination move an organization to a new understanding of itself. They can also assist how members are expected to work with each other over time. Both the trainer and the leader must disrupt the automatic processing mode of those being developed. Otherwise we can too easily revert back to what's comfortable and seemingly appropriate based on old standards and norms.

Well-known consultant and author James Champy asks: "Who would you follow into battle: the manager who spouts the vision thing, reads from the company's press releases, and feigns passion as the ship is sinking? Or the manager who displays empathy and understands how his behavior affects success or failure? The latter are those that lead to sustained greatness."

To disrupt one's automatic thinking process is certainly a big challenge. However, we bet you have had some experience doing this and can now leverage it in creating your desired possible self. For example, when you have traveled to a different culture (including within the same country), no doubt you have experienced going from automatic processing of knowing how things worked to a more controlled processing mode. In the different culture, you had to stop and take notice that it might take months, if not years, to develop deep trust. In addition, the different culture might make you pause when you question authority, or proactively break traditional rules that no longer serve any useful purpose. Instead of automatic processing, while experiencing cultural shock you had to stop and examine every step in the process in minute detail before you could take any actions.

There are many other possible examples, besides another culture, that you may have experienced. For instance, taking on a new assignment or participating in a social gathering for the first time. These rich experiences can be drawn from, and contribute to, your ALD. They can provide moments for you to break out of your automatic mode and into a controlled approach leading to your possible self.

Recently, a young, bright executive working in a telecommunications company told Bruce that she seemed unable to develop good working relationships with the executives from the company that had acquired her company. She felt, over time, she had built very strong and positive relationships with the previous all-male senior management team. However, she now noticed (going from automatic to controlled processing) that in the meetings with the new executive team, her comments were politely received, but never acted upon.

This recent experience became a wake-up call for her actual self-awareness. This moment had her wondering if she had to change the way she presented herself. Or, was it the new executives who needed to change, and/or both? She felt they had marginalized her and labeled her in stereotypic fashion. She was convinced that her opinion was either being ignored or discounted. She had taken a step backward, and realized that she was acting the same way as she did when she first started her career. That is, her actual self was as it had been in the past. However, in these new conditions, this old self was not working for her in terms of being truly heard and influencing this new group of leaders.

This situation represents for us an ideal opportunity for ALD, albeit real, but very difficult. The challenge points, not yet fully identified, deal with how to help this fledgling leader move from her actual self to a possible one she feels good about. Furthermore, she has to make sure that the other executives in the company will respect her possible self as well. Obviously, this new group of executives from a different culture may bring their own stereotypic views of women into their leadership roles. They will not change easily. Knowing this, how should this young female executive proceed?

If she is going to get the new leaders to respect her views, what is her own responsibility for changing? The others are in a higher position of power and they undoubtedly won't change. They are probably even unaware of the impact they are having on her. She certainly cannot just abandon her core values, but she may have to invoke some new pragmatic strategies in her possible self.

As an example of moving to her possible self, she may proactively attempt to manage her new bosses by contingently reinforcing—giving them recognition or attaining a successful outcome—any time (even slightly at first) they do truly seem to listen to her or act on her advice. ALD does not always have to be some ideal search for truth and goodness. In cases like this one, it may be as simple as reinforcing desirable "right" behavior. If all else fails, she may have to leave the field (take another job) to remain true to herself—and the others involved as well.

These are the types of critical challenges that we feel represent ALD experiences and moments. They don't come from the made-up cases or fabricated exercises so commonly found in training programs. Rather, they are real challenges that confront people like the young woman above. You can either grow from these situations or retreat from them.

All leaders have to constantly address dilemmas that challenge who they really are and what they want to become over time. In other words, as we have said many times, ALD requires meeting the challenges presented by both negative and positive moments. In fact, a recent survey reported by Cornell research psychologist Elaine Wethington found that among men and women who learned something upsetting about themselves, about half of the large sample also said they learned something good about themselves.

Our goal from the outset of this book has been to get you focused on taking advantage of and leveraging the challenges that arise. Where appropriate, you need to create the challenges for yourself before they become a serious dilemma. Specifically, one of the essential qualities of successful ALD is being flexible and adaptive.

Change will occur in terms of what leaders are expected to take on, what followers desire, and what competitors (inside and outside the organization) will dream up to challenge the leader. To address these changes and resulting challenges, the leader must be adaptive, and that involves a range; that is, not being merely adaptive or unwilling to adapt. The range of events or moments we confront can be categorized three ways: as triggers, jolts, and challenging dilemmas. Let's look at them.

Trigger Moments

These are negative or positive incidents that get us to think about who we are and what we do. They may not seem so consequential when they occur, but over time, as we think more about what happened, we go deeper into thinking about ourselves.

Richard Nixon did such self-analysis of the trigger events that resulted in his infamous style of leadership. Soon after he resigned from the presidency, while reminiscing with former aide Kenneth Clawson about his distrustful, angry style, he said:

> What starts the process, really, are the laughs and snubs and slights you get when you are a kid . . . But if you are reasonably intelligent and if your anger is deep enough and strong enough, you learn that you can change those attitudes by excellence, personal gut performance . . . [When you get to the top] you find you can't stop playing the game the way you've always played it . . . so you are lean and mean and resourceful and you continue to work on the edge.

Unfortunately, Nixon was apparently unable to turn his negative trigger moments in his childhood into positives. He did not change his automatic processing into controlled processing, leading to a better possible self. We would argue this inability or unwillingness to move from his actual self to his possible self inhibited his ALD, and the rest is history.

Jolts

Although somewhat just a play on words, we do feel a distinction can and should be made between what we refer to as a trigger moment and what we are calling a jolt. Unlike trigger events, a jolt is an event or moment that you know, when you experience it, has had an impact on you.

Frequently in the past, jolting events in terms of leadership development were associated with some crisis or, in the extreme, a tragedy. Most people love to discuss how terrible events have been translated into growth experiences that made them better people. For example, when we recently asked a police chief we know, who had dealt with thousands of cases over his long career, what event or moment defined his leadership, he replied without hesitation: "You know, I have not really discussed this before, but I know it was [he gave a precise date] when a colleague and friend of mine [he gave the name] was shot and killed in the line of duty." Unsolicited, he then went on to tell us another specific jolt he had when calling on a father to tell him his daughter had just been murdered—again giving us names of the father and victim and the precise date.

We don't dismiss this line of thinking and believe that it characterizes a portion of the range we describe as ALD. But what's often missing, as with this police chief, are the positive jolts that also shape who we are. Although often overlooked by people, we believe positive jolts can profoundly impact movement from our actual to our possible self.

We are not just talking about some accolade or award you received. A positive jolt may be as simple as seeing an uplifting film, observing a stranger help someone in need, or meeting someone who has an extraordinarily positive impact on you. You need to be more aware of these positive jolts that can set a new standard for your own conduct in the future. Positive as well as negative jolts can move you to your possible self in ALD.

By the way, the same police chief in the above example, when prompted, described how he brought his department into the future of technology. He was getting a cup of coffee one day and ran into the civil engineer next door to his office. The engineer asked him to come into his office so he could show him a new program he was working on. This was back in 1978. The engineer had designed a geographical map on his computer that allowed you to focus in on a particular bridge in the state, click on it, and all this information would pop up on the screen: its serial numbers, the year it was built, the last time it was resurfaced, etc.

The chief realized in that moment that the engineer had more information on the bridge than his officers had while going into a difficult, often dangerous, situation in a house. The responding officer often does not know who lives there, whether they have a license for a gun, whether there are warrants for anyone's arrest, or other pertinent details when confronting a dangerous situation. With this context, in that moment the chief was determined to bring the future he saw into the present by advancing the most aggressive campaign to integrate technology into police work. In 2004 the city police force he leads had one of the safest communities in the nation for a midsize city, with a one (his city) to three (other cities of similar size) ratio of officers needed to do their police work.

Challenging Dilemmas

Although the word "dilemma" tends to have a negative connotation, there are many dilemmas that can be leveraged and facilitate ALD. Some great leaders actually argue that they would deliberately create dilemmas for their followers in order to encourage them, in our terminology, to move from automatic to controlled processing. In particular, when you have had a consistent record of success, it is always helpful to have a leader pose a dilemma that makes you question the basic assumptions of how and why you are successful and what you may need to change to remain so.

As an example, CEO Jim Clifton, the leader of Gallup, in his state of the company address coming off a record-setting year of success, challenged his "co-leaders" to "reinvent" the company. This challenging dilemma served as a moment for us, as well as many of the other co-leaders we talked with over the years.

Like this successful leader at Gallup, we would argue it is much better for us to self-impose such dilemmas than to wait for our

competition to provide them for our learning experience. In fact
this year Clifton began with a personal story about Polaroid, which
recently ceased to exist as a company. He relayed how when he first
met his wife: that they attended a party at her place of work, which
was Polaroid. He was impressed at the time with the motivation
and capabilities of this group. He then indicated to his audience
that in the past week one of his employees put a cell phone in his
face, and afterward he realized his picture had been taken. He told
the audience that he tried to go back and imagine himself telling
the CEO of Polaroid, 30 years ago, that his fancy new technology
would be supplanted by a thing called a PC, or even a wireless phone.
He then encouraged his entire group of employees to make sure they
questioned their basic business assumptions in order not to fall into
the same traps as the once innovative, highly successful Polaroid.

FOR YOU TO DO IN YOUR ALD JOURNEY

We want you to identify one negative and one positive trigger, jolt,
and dilemma in your life that you feel (maybe upon reflection) has
positively accelerated your leadership development. In reflecting
back on these negative and positive triggers, jolts, and dilemmas,
address the following specific questions:

1. First, give a brief overall description of how it started, what
   happened, and how it ended.
2. What did you observe in yourself? In others?
3. What did you feel?
4. How did you react?
5. What did you learn?
6. What was the initial outcome?
7. If you changed, what was the longer-term outcome?
8. How did it impact your view of yourself?

In summary, though traditional leadership development programs have not specifically articulated this goal, the intent of our proposed ALD is to first understand your actual self and the move to the possible, more authentic and effective one. Once you recognize the gap, and the area you need to address to narrow and eventually close it, you send it to the future to see what it looks like. Then you need to bring this future back in order to work on making it a reality for your new, more authentic actual self.

LEADERSHIP NOTES

- *We are wired to process a lot of information automatically based on what we have learned in the past.* One way to enhance self-awareness is to force yourself to move from automatic to controlled processing. You give yourself time to reflect on how you felt, thought, and behaved.

- *Like learning any new hobby or sport, leadership is a complex process that requires tremendous self-discipline to learn.* You need to pick the areas you are going to focus on in terms of moving from the actual to the possible self, and then stay focused on those areas until you fully understand what you have done, or are doing, and what you want to do.

- *Leaders are on stage all of the time as "instructors" showing people around them how to behave.* Two of the most powerful ways that followers learn is by what the leader models for them and through what is called "vicarious learning." The leader has to remain self-aware that what they do is something that followers will believe is the right thing to do and will emulate.

6

TAKING THE RIGHT FORK IN THE ROAD: WHEN TO STAY THE COURSE AND WHEN TO CHANGE

THE COMPLEXITY of ALD thickens when we consider that on the one hand followers admire leaders who "stick to their guns," stay the course, but on the other, they also want their leaders to face up to realities, admit mistakes, and change directions or even reverse course. A spoof on public radio a year ago referred to leaders who had what was termed "functional executive disorder." What they meant by this was leaders who were so focused on performance outcomes that they lost track of the meaning of their work and their impact on others.

How can we avoid such dysfunctional leadership behavior but still deliver on conflicting demands? Today's shareholders and followers seem to want it both ways from their leaders. Unfortunately, most leaders tend to face this fork in the road of staying the course or changing directions and, as Yogi Berra said, simply take it.

An important part of the ALD process is, first of all, to recognize and understand when a critical juncture is reached. Then, once at this fork in the road, how do you effectively resolve when to stick with the current course and when to change directions? That is, how do you know when to take the "right" fork, not just, as Yogi said, "Take it."

Notice that we're talking about direction and course of action, not core values and beliefs. An important attribute of authentic leaders is that they maintain their transparent core values and beliefs. However, they also know when to stick with and when to change directions and their course of action. This chapter digs a bit deeper than the others in trying to unravel this complex dilemma in the ALD process. We will start with the role of self-identity.

THE ROLE SELF-IDENTITY PLAYS

Social psychologists have found that people tend to stick to a particular course of action to the extent it is tied to what is called their "self-identity." What this means is that the most powerful form of control individuals maintain over their course of action works from the inside out.

If you view yourself (i.e., your self-identity) as someone who depends on what others think in order to make your decisions, then you will regulate how you make your decisions based on the input gathered from others. On the other hand, if your self-identity can be characterized as independent, flexible, and adaptable, you'll be more willing and likely to choose a different course of action. Thus, self-identity provides the guideposts for how we regulate what we do and, equally important, what we choose not to do. Your self-identity will largely determine which fork in the road you choose—to stay or change.

THE NARRATIVE SELF

In Toni Morrison's commencement address to the Wellesley College graduating class of 2004, she stated, "Contrary to what you may have heard or learned, the past is not done and it is not over, it's still in process, which is another way of saying that when it's critiqued and analyzed, it yields new information about itself." We believe the same is true about your past. How you narrate the past to others tells you and them the type of past you want it to represent.

We are all authors of our own life paths. How we develop and write the script determines how others view us, and indeed how we view ourselves. Everyone is their own author, but some are more cognizant of being the author of their lives than others. Being the narrative author of one's life path requires, as we noted at the outset of this book, a keen awareness of the evolving self, including one's past. It also involves an engagement with followers, which helps to shape the narrative created by a leader.

Leaders who receive little if any feedback from followers will create a narrative of themselves that may be very different from what they would author if they did receive feedback. For instance, think back to the CEOs we described who don't know what is going on in their organizations.

Apart from followers providing feedback, leaders also come across accidental, fortuitous events that help shape what happens next thereafter. Fortuitous trigger events can change the whole course of one's life script or story, and that of others as well.

Looking through many biographies of world-class leaders, it's remarkable how many came to their positions through fortuitous events or circumstances. Arnold Schwarzenegger would be an example. A series of fortuitous events propelled him from what *Time* magazine called "a steroid munching, big-grinned, Austrian body builder into Hollywood stardom and then the governorship of the most populous state in the U.S." Only fortuitous triggers in his life could have made him into such an American cultural and political icon.

Although not as dramatic as this example, while authoring one's life, it is likely that the life path you pursue will take different courses, depending upon the fortuitous trigger events that emerge in the life stream. Setting oneself up to take advantage of those fortuitous events through self-reflection is a critical piece of life's ALD program.

During one-on-one chats with participants after many of our talks or programs, we commonly hear something like: "If you could only get our boss to view this initiative as something worth sticking to, I would be able to do what you suggest and achieve what I at least would like to accomplish." Part of the problem with these participants' leaders is that they have often developed a certain set of core beliefs about the direction they're pursuing. When you do talk with them, it's apparent that their beliefs are so strong that it is extremely difficult to change how they regulate their actions and decisions. Their story line has become largely fixed or anchored in a set of beliefs.

Even if you can get the leaders to agree to go against or suspend these deeply held values and beliefs, getting them to pursue another narrative, a course with which they are not identified, becomes an enormous challenge. Our presidents during both the Vietnam and Iraq wars come quickly to mind. However, so would the leaders of large and small businesses facing a decline in their core product-lines, or college administrators faced with relatively decreasing enrollment in humanities classes. We would again argue that this is where the "moments that matter" in their ALD come into play.

Specifically, when leaders set out to change a fundamental course they've been pursuing, they are changing how they define their "actual self," and the concurrent narrative about themselves that was created. After changing how they define their actual self—or self-identity—it then takes time, practice, and considerable discipline to learn how to view oneself differently. This means the self they are functioning with becomes more provisional. Moreover, without sufficient support, it's easy for even the most seasoned leaders to stray from good intentions. They may revert back to the self that had a deeper installed base, one that is ingrained in their actual self.

An interesting example of the role that self-identity plays in the process of when to stick and when to change arose in a workshop that Bruce recently conducted for the well-known Brookings Institution in Washington, D.C. The group consisted of a mix of middle-to senior-level federal officials who ranged in age from their early 30s to early 60s. At one of the workshop breaks, a participant discussed the challenge he saw in today's federal agencies in getting different cohorts to "identify" with new initiatives. He indicated that the now quite "experienced" federal employees who came in during President Kennedy's brief administration and during Johnson's subsequent "Great Society" years saw government as a key solution to societal problems. Conversely, employees who entered federal service under Presidents Nixon and Reagan saw government as more of a facilitator, not a director, or the solution, to problems and challenges. These very different models and narratives for federal service resulted in each age group cohort identifying with different ways to look at and approach the same problems. Often, the result was conflict within the ranks.

Our self-identity is shaped by moments, and it then shapes how we experience the future moments that arise in our life path.

Simply asking those who identified with the politics of one era to switch and adapt their thinking and behavior to the orientation of another era is no trivial undertaking. Such an ingrained self-identity story is what leaders are challenged with day in and day out as they wrestle with whether to change or stay the course.

Just imagine how difficult it is for Palestinian leaders to change their youth's view of Israel if they want to resolve their differences and settle on a peace agreement. For much of their lives, many Palestinians have identified with the Intifada. Changing direction is changing what they have come to strongly identify with over their life span. It is part of their collective narrative.

Those who understand paradigmatic change—such as major changes in scientific thinking, from a flat world to a round world, or Newtonian physics to quantum physics—know that those engrossed in the old paradigm, when confronted with the new paradigm, do not "get it" or cannot even "see" the new paradigm. One reason is that old paradigm thinkers have so much invested in that narrative, they can't let go. Those who study paradigm shifts know it is better to start the new paradigm with a "clean slate." In other words, those with little or no experience in the old paradigm, or in our terms, those who do not have their self-identity based on and tied so tightly to the old paradigm, are more receptive to the new paradigm.

Applying what we know about paradigm shifts to the ALD process, or what fork in the road to choose, leaders first have to be self-aware. They have to understand their self-identity and where it comes from. Then, when appropriate, they can put in place the mechanisms that will help them regulate to a new "operating system," paradigm, or story.

FORCES THAT AFFECT STAYING THE COURSE OR CHANGING

Generally, as we noted above, we expect and admire leaders who are consistent and stay the course—except if the course is clearly wrong. Such consistent leaders are able to express who they are across divergent situations. Unfortunately, however, many leaders adopt the stay-the-course strategy even when it is wrong.

One reason for sticking to the wrong course is what social psychology has identified as "escalation of commitment." Simply put, this means that the more individuals have invested in pursuing a particular goal or direction, the less likely it is that they'll pull back and set a new direction. This escalation is due to their "sunk costs," or investments in the direction already pursued. It's a process akin to a novelist who gets to the last chapter and then suddenly realizes that he wants to change the whole story line. Do you think he'd completely rewrite the book? Obviously, with his sunk costs, this would be very hard to do.

This concept of escalation of commitment can be readily observed by people who invest in the stock market. Historical events also provide rich examples. Bruce discovered as much when he visited Sweden several years ago to do a presentation on leadership at the Royal Military Academy.

While visiting with one of the professors from the academy in his office one evening, he noticed a chart on the wall with a broad black line that became increasingly thinner as it went from left to right across the chart. The line went all the way across and then back again, reversing course, becoming thinner and thinner, until it was pencil thin. Bruce asked his colleague what the chart represented, and was told that it showed graphically the number of men in Napoleon's army who started their ill-fated invasion of Russia and his losses over time, until he'd almost lost his entire army.

Inspecting this visual chart of Napoleon's defeat clearly indicated significant points in the series of battles and mishaps where this great military leader should have cut his losses and returned to France. He obviously didn't, nor did Hitler a century and a half later, when he blundered in also trying to invade Russia. Both intransigent courses of action demonstrate great, or tragic, historical examples of the escalation of commitment.

If Napoleon had studied and understood the psychological concept of escalation of commitment, would he have changed course, and would the history of the world have changed dramatically? We don't know, of course, but such a learning moment for Napoleon is interesting to at least contemplate. Just as it's interesting to contemplate how fortuitous events shape the subsequent events that shape our own life story or narrative.

Here is another such story: A young professional on a plane flying back from China entered into a conversation with a more established businessman on work, career, and life. By the time the flight was half over, they had both agreed that the fortuitous event that brought them together in two seats next to one another set in motion a relationship they both wanted to continue past the immigration gates in Chicago. In fact, as the plane was landing, the younger man asked the older one if he would entertain serving as his mentor, and the older man readily agreed. They exchanged contacts before leaving, and had a meaningful, productive relationship through the years.

One never knows when such important fortuitous events will arise, and how to regulate oneself in getting through that event and the subsequent ones it influences or creates. Certainly, you must be aware that such events are worth exploring. Then the key becomes how to take advantage of them so they remain essential ingredients in life's authentic leadership development program.

All leaders—not just military leaders—need to know when to adjust or completely change their course. These changes can occur in terms of their own development, other people's development, and ultimately the challenges they take on and pursue over time. In part, this is why it's so important to focus on enhancing the self-awareness of leaders and, in turn, their self-identity. Without such self-knowledge, there can be no course corrections when either fortuitous or negative events arise.

In our daily lives, we invest a great deal in developing who we are and what we become. We make this investment in both substance and image through the narratives we create for ourselves and others. There will come a time when one is "jolted" into change, or confronted with a "moment that matters." And these jolts or moments will no doubt change the narrative one creates for his or her life.

Under our own radar screens we create narratives about the ways things should be, and then we follow the script until we're triggered or jolted into self-awareness.

Jolts or moments should cause deep reflection on the course we embark upon and that we set in motion. For many, the costs of changing are just too steep. Also, the time available may be viewed as insufficient.

An example would be a young lawyer at the World Bank who told Bruce recently that she was saddened by what had happened to her father. This elderly Russian had, throughout his entire life, fully identified with what he believed were the ideals of communism. When the Berlin Wall came down and the Soviet empire broke up, for his daughter, who was just beginning to emerge, it was an opportunity to move in a completely new life direction— one in which she would become a lawyer in the United States. In contrast, her father felt that he did not have the capacity to make such a life course change. At present, disillusioned, but not able or willing to give up his self-identity, he was slipping further and further into a state of helplessness and depression. She described him as being merely a shell of his former self.

In our terms, the elderly Russian had consciously lost his self-identity of being a communist. His storytelling (i.e., his narrative script) appeared to be over. He was not able to change his life's course. The old narrative persisted in the new realities he was confronting, and it created tremendous discord.

What we build up on the inside, in terms of coordinating our core beliefs and values, is often difficult to disentangle later in life, when it might be opportune, or essential, to change the course. Whether this old communist, or today's leaders undergoing ALD, one must stay the course or change, from the inside out.

A PARADOX FACING ALD

For ALD, being a consistently strong, decisive leader must be weighed against being adaptive, flexible, and transforming. These countervailing forces or tradeoffs are what constitute one of the great paradoxes facing ALD.

When do authentic leaders stay the course to build the confidence and admiration of followers, and when do they redirect the course to gain the same respect? When the present course is clearly wrong, the costs outweigh the present or future benefits, and/or it is unethical or hurtful, then changing the course becomes relatively easy. However, what about when it is not so clear-cut?

Iwao Tomita is a semiretired accountant working for Deloitte Touche Tohmatsu in Japan. Tomita is known for his fierce independence and willingness to take on the established power brokers. Today, he has set a course to push the Japanese government to enact laws that will create a more transparent environment for business transactions. Tomita indicates that in Japan the CPAs are not asking the companies the "difficult questions" that need to be asked to assure transparency and accurate reporting of their books.

Most often, leaders are faced with shades of gray, dilemmas or tradeoffs, not black and white, right or wrong distinctions in their choices. The paradox that these leaders are confronting is that they have to ask their followers to stop believing in what they worked so hard to get them to believe in from the outset.

Pursuing a significant redirection takes as much courage and confidence as staying the course. It also takes the support and trust of followers to be fully successful. In addition, one always runs the risk of being seen as inconsistent.

A common example regarding this paradox is the significant investment that many of today's organizational leaders are making in large information technology systems. Corporate and public sector leaders are contemplating or making huge expenditures on brand new information technology platforms to replace what are referred to as "legacy systems." Unfortunately, these costly, often career-defining interventions, like mergers and acquisitions, hover at a failure rate of around two-thirds.

Now, what chief information officer (CIO) wants to go to his or her CEO and say, "After $10 million of investment in a new IT platform, I am convinced that any more investment in this initiative is throwing money down a rat hole!" To the contrary, time and again we see not only CIOs, but many other organizational, community, and national political leaders, become so committed to a particular, often costly direction that they simply believe they can no longer change course. (Remember our discussion of escalation of commitment?) Paradoxically, these situations often represent a red flag signal of when one should "cut bait" and change course. Or at least these should signal the need to consider a broader set of options or different pathways to accomplish the desired end goal.

When leaders commit an ethical violation, it's often because they have made an ill-advised decision to stay the course instead of changing direction. As they move down the slippery slope of an ethical dilemma, they may begin to take action that covers the problem, with the hope that it will not be uncovered.

These questionable ethics can be found with many of the so-called "Barons of Bankruptcy." This is the title of a recent study by the *Financial Times* that found leaders of the 25 largest business failures walking away with over $3.3 billion in pay and gains from selling their stock. However, from an authentic leader perspective, making a course correction might have cost them at least short-term personal gain, but might have also saved their companies and all other stakeholders from being devastatingly wiped out.

It's not only these high-profile leaders of bankrupt firms; we see, again and again, how leaders from all walks of life define themselves by the actions they have taken. To change course suggests a change in how they define who they are, or their self-identity.

The more we wrap ourselves in our choices, the more difficult it becomes to sever the tie and take a different direction. This occurs not just in terms of the choices we have made with business strategies and investments, but also in our relationships with people. Whom you select for a job opening, the person you mentor, whom you socialize with in and outside the organization, all involve choices and psychic investment. Although we want our leaders to be identified with a particular cause or direction, we also want them to have the wisdom to change course when the situation warrants such a change.

Many would say that President Johnson during the Vietnam War had so tied himself to his commitment to liberate the country from communism that increasingly it became "Johnson's war," not America's. Over time it consumed him and his presidency. Johnson feared what his constituency would think if he was to retreat from the war, in effect claiming defeat.

It takes courage to stay the course and be persistent, and it takes wisdom to know when your losses exceed the point where it no longer makes sense to pursue a particular course of action. It takes a degree of bravery to admit a mistake has been made, and to stop and change course.

A recent geopolitical example of not changing course would be the stand President Robert Mugabe has taken in Zimbabwe. Most knowledgeable observers agree that he has almost single-handedly caused the collapse of a once thriving economy and vibrant African nation. He simply has no intention, or even capacity, for relinquishing his ruthless power grip on this struggling country. He has refused to change course at a time where all the signs point in the direction of the value of democratizing his country.

A contrasting example of the results of staying the course in this difficult part of the world might be found in Luisa Diogo, the first female prime minister of Mozambique. She is largely given credit for resisting the corrupt powers in charge and rescuing this African country devastated by civil war, floods, soaring HIV/AIDS infection rates, and a collapsed economy. Through her leadership, recently characterized in a *Time* article by transparency, accountability, and good governance, she has stayed the course and earned the respect of her followers and the world community, as recognized by the World Bank and the United Nations. Her performance impact has been unmistakable—remarkable economic growth rates and doubling the per capita income of Mozambique over the past decade.

Another example of an unwillingness to change course has been elucidated by some of the leaders in NASA. A recent director, Sean Okeefe (who now heads Louisiana State University), indicated in a public speech on C-Span that it was primarily the traditional culture of NASA that contributed to the second space shuttle disaster (the *Columbia*). He felt there was a clear unwillingness among many NASA leaders to share needed, relevant information to make the best decisions.

After the first disaster, when the *Challenger* had blown up, many felt that the problems in NASA were not technical so much as due to the agency's leadership and culture. Yet many of the same issues that came to light in the hearings around the *Challenger* many years before also arose again when the *Columbia* had a meltdown upon reentry on February 1, 2003. The NASA leaders in the decision chain of the *Columbia* mission had not sufficiently changed course after the lessons learned from the earlier *Challenger* problems.

Part of the problem may be that NASA project managers decide whether or not a ship goes up in space. Unlike the nuclear navy, there is no independent technology advisory committee at NASA that provides opinion and oversight. In the Navy, if the independent technology committee says the ship doesn't sail due to some potential technology problem, the captain is simply not allowed to sail. NASA has apparently created a culture and system of evaluation that does not allow for such independent evaluation, which potentially leads to decisions that on the surface may make business sense, or political face-saving, but are clearly not safe.

Often, we escalate our commitment to actions that no longer serve the needs or aspirations of our organizations.

Again, every leader, not just those highlighted in newsworthy events, is at some point confronted with the challenge of facing a fork in the road and confronting the decision of whether or not to change. In some instances this may require a transformation to a whole new way of operating that fundamentally goes against the investments already made and the direction set. Prior to these transformative moments, we must prepare ourselves—and those around us—to at least entertain the possibility of change; to have the credibility to suggest that changing course should at least be considered a possibility.

If you are the leader, sensitivity to possible change involves creating the conditions where people will be willing to tell you when the signs point to a new direction being needed. This is why we feel it's so important for the leader to create an engaged culture. A culture where people feel there is an open, transparent climate. A culture where dissent is not only permitted, but with sufficient reinforcements for airing one's most critical views with others in the group and with the leader. We especially must create climates that deter self-deception, as well as the deception of others. Let us give a poignant example.

Recently, Bruce sat in with a group of union leaders and management staff. They had urgently come together in order to try to save about a thousand manufacturing jobs. This embattled but unfortunately typical, well-known firm had gone through five different transitions in ownership over the course of its history. It had gone from being one of the most venerable names in all of American business to one in which employees had to say, "I work for a company called 'Blah,' which used to be called . . ."

One woman from the union's leadership spoke to the issue of identity by saying how much pride she used to have in telling people where she worked, and now they didn't even know the name of her new employer! Much of her own identity was tied to her well-known and respected former company, which is exactly what the leadership of this firm wanted to create. Now, the leaders faced the challenge of changing identity for themselves and their employees from something in which they all had become true believers.

The latest buyout of this company involved the potential for a positive future again, with the parent company willing to invest significant money in capital equipment in order to position them to become an enduring, competitive manufacturing facility. But both the managers and union leaders who had worked for the organization during the various transitions had a hard time believing in this latest positive vision. They had become accustomed to each new owner coming in with a "plan," or worse, what they called "a program," to once again transform the company into a successful manufacturing facility. To say the least, few in the room were buying yet another such course correction, and most thought of it as a deception. The weight of knowing full well that at least 20 percent of the workforce was not going to be there on this latest journey could not be overcome, even if the new vision was authentic.

For the union leadership, who had "been there and done that," management had lost all of its credibility and trustworthiness. Whatever the management team said was critically analyzed by the union leaders to understand its true intent. Rumors were running rampant among the rank-and-file of impending doom.

The new management team coming on board kept reiterating that "together" they could build a great future. On the other hand, the union and most employees still questioned why a particular department had been moved from one location to another, or why a plan for consolidating space was being drawn up. Tremendous energy, goodwill, time, and resources were being wasted because of the loss of authenticity of the firm's leaders.

Whether the positive future will actually come to pass may in large part be a function of the prior history of broken promises. These earlier promises were made by the previous owners and leaders, who had not invested in the long-term future of this manufacturing facility. Indeed, contributing to the organization's current woes is the fact that many of the existing employees in this facility had been "saved" by being moved there by the union in order to protect their jobs after the other facilities had been closed around the country. So, the remaining employees, who had survived up to five corporate takeovers, downsizing, and numerous plant closings, were on this last island of hope (or despair).

In many ways, the identities of these employees were tied to a glorious past that had not in truth existed for some time. However, most still defined themselves in terms of the old company. For example, when they met someone new, they would say: "I work for . . ., but it used to be that great company . . . " And then they'd supply the old name. Unfortunately, this sad tale has become the rule rather than the exception in the acquisition-and-merger-mad world we now have, and it heightens the challenges facing ALD.

GETTING BACK TO KNOWING YOURSELF

We began this chapter with throwing out the formidable challenge that faces all leaders: when to stay the course and when to change. It's the ultimate competing demand. So far, we have emphasized that it takes courage to change course, even when a course correction is the only viable strategy to pursue to secure either one's own future, or one's organization.

There are many pressures on leaders to stay the course, not the least of which is how they define themselves. We have seen that getting anyone to change their identity is no trivial undertaking. This is true whether it is on a death march through Russia, changing the core product lines we produce, or giving up one one's successful career to pursue something you truly enjoy and that better fits with your vision of your possible self. Hopefully, by now it has become clear to you why you must truly know yourself. Knowing who you are is the only true way to decide what needs to be changed.

Knowing yourself begins with knowing what your strengths and weaknesses are and why you are pursuing a particular course of action. Sometimes, this course no longer makes sense to you or anyone else who is honestly willing to share that information with you. Yet, as we discussed earlier in the book, such self-awareness rarely comes only from oneself.

Self-awareness often comes from others who are willing to say what they think about you, especially if you 're capable of listening attentively. Unfortunately, it's not uncommon for others to be observing attentively but speaking too softly for you to listen. This is where self-regulation has to enter into the ALD process.

GETTING BACK TO REGULATING THE SELF

As you have learned by now, the beginning point of any significant change rests within the person. So, as a leader, when you face the fork in the road, whether you change or not depends on your self-awareness of who you are and what you're interested in becoming over time.

Now, let's assume that you are aware of the change you want to make in yourself, or what we have called your "actual self." Let's assume you have the motivation and support to start the change process. To be successful in making the change requires self-regulation, which is your own personal process for keeping yourself on course.

To show the relevance to ALD, let's start with explaining what self-regulation means to sustain enduring change in organizations.

Throughout every day, there are many instances where we all can and sometimes do apply self-regulation.

Let's say that someone sends you a disturbing e-mail. Instead of firing back an emotional reply, you decide to wait 24 hours before responding. This deliberate delay has in effect become your "self-regulation rule." If in fact you follow such a rule after 24 hours has expired you might decide that an angry, negative response is unnecessary or unwise, which is often the case for many of us. You have just demonstrated self-regulated behavior. You establish and agree to follow some boundaries or guideposts. These provide the self-regulated direction you need to stay on course or to change. In other words, self-regulation provides the needed guidance in choosing the right fork to take in the road.

Think about the last time you were listening to someone share something of great importance to them, and possibly to you. However, you interrupted them, or you weren't listening as hard as you should have. It is in these moments where we lack the necessary discipline, or self-regulation. It is in these moments where the special relationship of trust between leaders and followers may begin to erode.

We have all had the experience of wanting to tell a leader something that was bothering us. However, when we broach the problem, the leader interrupts, telling us, "If you think you have it bad, well let me tell you my story . . ." and then he or she proceeds to do so. This represents poor self-regulation on the part of both the follower and the leader. Self-regulation allows us to get away from getting others' permission or affirmation for what we know is the right direction to take.

Self-regulation in the ALD process is based on the assumption that you know what you want to do with yourself vis-à-vis the direction you have set for your leadership. For that matter, the same is true for your followers. If you don't know yourself, then how can you proceed to regulate your own actions and behaviors with others?

You can, but you are not going to be very effective. You run the big risk of being perceived as inconsistent and therefore not trustworthy. You just "take" Yogi's fork in the road. In ALD you have to have a sense of self that highlights the areas you want to change, focus on, and regulate. You take the "right" fork in the road in terms of staying the course or changing.

Most of us go through our interactions with others day in and day out. We are able to maintain, or at least minimally regulate, our interactions. However, obviously there are times when we get off-track. For example, when we are distracted or under stress, we may say something we don't really mean. We may come down on the wrong side of an issue. We then have to go back and try to recover our relationship.

An example of being on the wrong side of an issue and trying to recover recently occurred when first-year Nebraska football Coach Bill Callahan, under extreme pressure from fans and the local media after a couple of losses, decided that to be more efficient, only those players seeing considerable action would be allowed on the field during pregame warm-ups. This not only broke with tradition and the whole team concept, but also drew a negative reaction from the first-team players and captains. They complained that this decision deprived the scout team players any chance to be part of the game-day experience, and "they work as hard as we do."

To Coach Callahan's credit, he tried to recover, to change course, by publicly admitting his error in judgment by stating in a news conference:

> I made a mistake. That's part of the growing process. To think that you don't make a mistake as a coach or a player, that's ludicrous. We're all going to have these trials and tribulations. Certainly those guys were deserving to be on the field. It was no disrespect. I explained that to our team.

The next day a sports reporter noted, "Kudos to the coach for realizing his mistake and not letting such a little thing fester into a big problem. He made a wrong decision, he listened, he corrected, and he apologized. End of story." The fans and players also greatly respected Callahan's reaction, and his stock went up in Nebraska's "Husker Nation," especially when the team won the next game with acknowledged "entire team intensity."

As Coach Callahan noted, it is simply not possible to engage in complex relationships and not make a mistake or have a misunderstanding that leaves someone upset. Yet most followers expect their leaders to "be on" all of the time. This includes not only coaches, but prominent senior leaders in all our organizations whom we may only formally meet and interact with infrequently, if at all. From these fleeting moments we often derive our impressions of our leaders. Although unfair, such leaders must maintain Six Sigma quality levels in all their interactions with others because these moments matter to followers in forming their perceptions of them.

One of the most desired behaviors of effective leaders is to "be in the moment" with their followers, focusing just on them in that moment.

Too often, the more senior and prominent leaders are, the less opportunity followers have to interact with them. Based on only a limited set of interactions, followers nevertheless tend to formulate their opinion of what their leaders stand for and who they represent. Accordingly, this requires a tremendous amount of discipline (self-regulation) by prominent leaders to present a consistent image of who they are and what they want to accomplish. This is why we suggest four simple guidelines to top leaders:

1. Keep your priorities simple.
2. Express and even flaunt your most important core value.

3. Clearly tell relevant others what your "red lines" or boundaries of acceptability are.
4. Stay as consistent as possible.

When faced with a fork in the road, following such simple rules of self-regulation will make it considerably easier to make the right choice. This is because your followers have come to trust your base of consistency. They will listen and accept when you feel it is appropriate to stay the course or make a correction or even introduce radical change.

To gain trust, the leader must have this capacity for self-regulation. This is the case when the leader is making major changes or just trying to stay on message, even when others are not supportive. The leader must be self-regulated to remain interested in what someone has to say, even after a frustrating 14-hour day. Again, self-regulation means being in control of yourself and the way you behave with others.

Self-regulation provides consistency for the leader and those he or she leads, and forms a basis for conditional trust and, over time, a deeper sense of internal trust. To demonstrate, simply think back to a leader in your life, one whose response you never knew in advance when you entered his office. There were times when he seemed totally interested in you, and other times when he indicated no apparent interest and even seemed rude.

All leaders have tempers and bad days. Unfortunately, this unpredictability on the part of the leader conditions followers to also self-regulate by not sharing information that they feel may trigger a bad reaction from the leader. It is an interesting paradox: Leaders' inconsistencies around self-regulation initiates a consistency in the self-regulation of followers to not share information with them. Again, the complexity of ALD thickens.

SELF-REGULATION AND AUTHENTICITY

People who are comfortable with themselves and know where their center lies seem to have an easier time of regulating their behavior. They can be more consistent. They are more likely to have positive interactions with followers as a consequence. This is because they're not constantly trying to figure out who they are while confronting inevitable questions, challenges, and criticisms.

Leaders who know themselves have much more energy to address what others say. They tend to listen more intently. They can reallocate considerable energy from solving their own self-development problems to developing others around them. Yet, despite these advantages, self-regulated leaders still naturally face a potential conflict of interest when it comes to dealing with others. Specifically, they may become frustrated and upset with someone or a group. However, if comfortably self-regulated, they may control that anger to allow time for the offending individual or group to change, or to accommodate a new way of doing things.

Of course, in most instances being in self-control is a good thing; it helps facilitate more positive interactions. Yet we have all met leaders and followers who never share with us their true feelings about any issue. Such dysfunctional, self-regulated behavior is not what we are advocating for leaders or followers who want to be viewed as authentic.

ALD requires that you set the "red zones" in which, if entered, your response is clear, swift, and appropriate. Those individuals who follow you must know what's unacceptable and acceptable as well as you do. For the gray area in between, you must establish where discussion and give-and-take seems appropriate and welcome. Without such boundaries it becomes difficult to establish an authentic relationship with others, and, importantly, to provide a solid basis for building trust.

As an example of establishing red zones, both of us have heard seasoned Gallup leaders say to new researchers: "You never screw with the data, because the data is the data, and simply report it." Think about how important that statement is to the authenticity of a company whose image counts on people believing that the data is truly valid. Without the integrity of the data, a company known for its measurement of opinions is ruined. As pointed out by the Warren Buffett example earlier in the book, the same applies to a business leader's integrity.

There are certain fundamental boundaries that all leaders have, or should have. These boundaries portray to others their authentic self. Knowing clearly what these red zones are helps to shape what people in an organizational unit, division, or entire company will later call "our culture." As Lincoln, Nebraska, sports reporter Brian Rosenthal observed about first-year football coach Callahan's admitted mistake discussed earlier, "Callahan is still learning about Nebraska's personality. He'll be learning for some time, too. No matter how much you study streaks and rivalries and traditions, you can't fully understand the culture until you've been a part of it for a while."

Going back to Buffett: When he sent the letter to his CEOs that they can tolerate financial loses, but not the loss of one shred of their company's integrity, he is spelling out the boundaries and cultural values of his firm, Berkshire Hathaway. He was indicating the importance of self-regulation around the high standards of business conduct he expects from himself and those who work for him. Specifically, he was saying that they should regulate their decision to tell him at the very first instance of awareness that something does not seem as it should be. Give him bad news that may in any way question the integrity of the company sooner than the good news, and he in turn would be an advocate for them in their situation.

In other words, Buffett made his red zones very clear, which has built for him a near bulletproof reputation for integrity in business practices.

The problem is that most leaders probably don't know themselves as well as Buffett knows himself. Therefore, when they come to a point where they should self-regulate, they often fail to do so. In fact, they may not even be self-aware enough to realize that they should be self-regulating.

The gap between self-awareness and self-regulation may be particularly evident in younger, less experienced leaders. They are often still trying to figure out who they are, and at the same time be successful enough to make visible progress and remain or grow in their leadership role. It may be, as we have suggested earlier, that they have escalated their commitment to a course or direction that is tightly connected to their own identity. If this is the case, it becomes difficult to decouple from a position and take the right fork. Again, ALD, in the deepest sense, rarely occurs alone, in isolation.

In the examples provided so far, you can see that self-regulation depends on being aware of one's self-concept. This is necessary, but not by itself sufficient. It is easier for leaders to self-regulate when they also have the support to do so—either based on the culture of their organization or respected others (top leaders or followers) who support them in the direction being pursued. Leaders pursue a course of action that they believe they will be reinforced for pursuing—either extrinsically (not necessarily pay, but more important, recognition and respect from valued others) or intrinsically through self-reinforcement.

Again, in ALD one starts from the inside (self-awareness and self-reinforcement) and works toward the outside (extrinsic reinforcement). However, we also know from research that perhaps the single biggest derailment factor in any leadership development is the lack of support from the organization we send people back to after training. For example, if the organization's top leadership is not aware of its pivotal role in supporting the change the newly trained leader has become aware of, there is an obvious problem. Even worse, if the top leadership is against any change, then upon reentry the trainee and the leadership program itself will be doomed to failure.

GETTING BACK TO SELF-EFFICACY

In Chapter 4 we introduced the role that self-efficacy can play in self-awareness. We said this psychological strength refers to the confidence that one will be successful in achieving a particular task or meeting particular challenges. Well-known social psychologist Albert Bandura more precisely defines self-efficacy as people's judgment or belief of how well they can execute the courses of action necessary to successfully deal with specific situations. Self-efficacy is different from self-esteem, which is how people generally feel about themselves. One can have high self-esteem, for example, but low self-efficacy on some specific tasks, such as running a computer program.

Those with high self-efficacy on a given task will choose to get involved, welcome the challenge; put forth the necessary effort to successfully accomplish the task; and persist when they encounter problems or obstacles. This self-efficacy is obviously based on past successes in the same or similar situations. However, efficacy should not simply be equated with success.

Building self-efficacy depends on how the person interprets success. If attaining success was too easy, or not the result of the individual's doing, then this would not contribute to efficacy. In addition to directly experienced success, efficacy can also be the result of watching relevant others succeed, receiving positive feedback, and being psychologically and physiologically aroused and healthy.

Applied to our discussion here, if leaders who come to the fork in the road have high self-efficacy, they tend to believe—they are confident—that the course being pursued is the right one. It has a sufficiently high probability of success. If successful, then leaders continue to build their efficacy, for what they are doing is demonstrably the right course of action. In their mind, they have established a particular probability of success. They have developed a level of self-efficacy concerning the particular dilemma, challenge, or opportunity being confronted. Their level of efficacy guides them as to whether to stay the course or change directions.

Considerable research has found that developing a leader's and follower's self-efficacy results in higher performance capacity. In fact, the meta-analysis of 114 studies conducted by Fred and Alex Stajkovic, mentioned in Chapter 4, found a higher average relationship between self-efficacy and work-related performance than other widely recognized techniques such as goal setting, work attitudes (job satisfaction), or personality traits (such as conscientiousness). In other words, the evidence is clear that highly efficacious people tend to be effective performers.

Because of this link to performance, the job of ALD is to help develop leadership efficacy. This means that you will come to believe and have confidence that you'll be more successful as a leader over time. Furthermore, in ALD you develop your self-efficacy for being challenged by yourself and others to change direction when such change is required. Put another way, you have to have self-efficacy for the change you make to become successful.

Building efficaciousness or confidence is again where the top leadership in an organization can help facilitate ALD. If top management has created a supportive climate in the past for making such changes, and rewarded you for successful changes, you will then feel more confident to make the latest change, and, significantly, to make it work.

When leaders take over in new situations, they are typically less confident. This can be explained in terms of their level of leadership efficacy, which is much lower than when they were in a situation they understood and had success dealing with in the past.

Part of the challenge for accelerating ALD faster than life's program is to develop leader efficacy to take on new challenges and opportunities that have not yet resulted in directly experienced success. If we can build leaders' efficacy in new situations more rapidly, the research evidence clearly indicates they, and their followers, will ultimately be more successful.

This efficacy building can also be accomplished through vicarious and modeling procedures (which we will discuss in the final chapter). This process does not require leaders to directly experience the success themselves. Yet, as we previously noted in our discussion of escalation of commitment and other such problems, leaders often will inflate their estimates of probable success while facing clear indicators that it should be time to cut one's losses and turn in a new direction. Another way to put it is that leaders must be aware of, and self-regulate against, the dangers of false efficacy. We never said that ALD would be straightforward and easy to accomplish.

CREATING THE CONDITIONS FOR FOLLOWER INPUT

The roller-coaster environment we described earlier in the example of the manufacturing facility undergoing successive changes in ownership is not that unusual today. Indeed, we have both marveled at how much you can learn in a short visit to an organization. An inauthentic culture about an organization's views on its leadership may quickly surface.

Bruce recently experienced this inauthentic culture while conducting a series of meetings with employees throughout one day. In almost all instances, the door would be open at the beginning of the interaction, but then the individual or a member of the group would run over and deliberately close the door whenever they had something "confidential" to say.

So much of the information appeared to be filtered in this real-world organizational example that it was nearly impossible to get a read on what people actually thought about their leaders—unless the door was closed. This might help explain why a number of the senior managers had no less than two or sometimes three outside coaches who were working with them on leadership. We are certainly not against the use of coaching. However, it appeared that these multiple coaches were substituting for friends, colleagues, and, most of all, followers who could tell their leaders the truth about how they behaved with them. The organization appeared to be "outsourcing" the needed support and upward communication to these outside coaches.

A major characteristic of authentic leaders is that they create the conditions in which followers can be open and transparent with them. Given the results we presented in the poll on leadership in Chapter 2, it is clear that most leaders today need to work a lot harder to encourage followers to tell them what they truly think about their direction, decisions, interactions, trust level, and so forth.

This challenge of getting followers to open up was vividly portrayed in the popular film a few years ago, *Master and Commander*, starring Russell Crowe. As the major theme in the movie, Crowe's character, a British naval commander, became hell-bent on pursuing a French ship that had successfully attacked and partially disabled his ship. The French ship was a more formidable vessel in terms of size and gunnery. The commander appears to have become obsessed with catching the French ship, and displays a high degree of leader efficacy. This confidence was based on the many prior battles he had won as a commander.

In a key scene in the movie—the moment that mattered in the commander's ALD—his closest friend, the ship's surgeon, passionately relays the difficulty the followers are having with his present, seemingly nonrational, course of action. They fear it may lead to potentially catastrophic results. The surgeon asks the commander if he has permission to speak as his friend or, he asks, must he speak as a subordinate. The commander gives him permission to speak as his friend. The surgeon then proceeds to detail the commander's blind obsession; as a friend, he gets him to reflect on the questionable, personal course he is pursuing. In our terms, the follower helped the leader become more self-aware of his commitment to a wrong course of action.

In this movie scene, we can see the leader specifically giving permission to his follower to be transparent and tell what he believes is information he needs to hear. In most organizations, the giving of permission is not as literal, but may still take a lot of courage, time, and effort on the part of the leader to be successful.

Creating conditions for authentic input from followers requires leaders to be self-aware and confident enough to be open to being challenged. This holds true even on the leader's most tried and true assumptions. Followers must be given the space and comfort level to challenge the leader. Thus, like the leader, followers must develop their own level of efficacy and authenticity.

Through transparency in their culture, leaders are in charge of creating the conditions to learn what they don't know.

Followers continually ask themselves: How successful will I be in getting the leader to listen to me? What are the potential costs if I fail to do so, for me personally and for our group and organization? In order for followers to feel enabled to "tell it like it is," the leader must build the followers' confidence or efficacy. To the followers, there must be a high probability of success that if they challenge leaders, the leaders will listen, reflect, and at least consider, appreciate, and respect what they have to say.

This openness to listen, this transparency, has to be there, even if the leader then does nothing about it. On the other hand, if leaders never provide the opportunity to listen to followers, or do not listen or reinforce that followers should come to them, what impact do you think that will have on their followers' level of self-efficacy? They simply will not have the confidence to come forward, and as a consequence, the leader would be shutting off perhaps the most vital source of needed information on taking the right fork in the road.

DIFFERENT TYPES OF EFFICACY IN ALD

Self-efficacy applies to specific challenges, problems, and opportunities that one faces over time. As we have seen in Chapter 4, where "means efficacy" (having the right tools) and "collective efficacy" (the power of group confidence) was introduced, this important psychological capacity of self-efficacy can take many different forms. They can be applied and have powerful implications for resulting performance. Here are some examples of different types of efficacies that are particularly relevant to ALD:

- High moral efficacy: I have confidence in taking a stand on what I believe is ethically the right thing to do.
- High leader efficacy: I have confidence in assuming and effectively carrying out my leadership role.
- High follower efficacy: I am confident in doing my job effectively and, if need be, can go to my leader to discuss anything.
- High task efficacy: I have confidence that I can do a specific task successfully.

Although Bandura's original conception of efficacy was task specific, there is increasing theory-building and research findings that leaders in particular may develop a high level of what is called "general efficacy." This means that a leader's efficacy or confidence in being successful may at least generalize across a domain of similar situations. For example, a leader may have high general efficacy for developing followers into becoming leaders. Such general efficacy allows the leader's confidence to "broaden and build" (just like positive emotions have been shown to do).

Combined with the fact that efficacy can be developed— through experienced success, vicariously and modeling successful relevant others, verbal persuasion and positive feedback, and psychological and physiological arousal and wellness—we hope you see why we have given so much attention to this relatively sophisticated but often overlooked psychological strength.

ALD built around specific and general efficacy provides leaders with a stronger base to feel confident that if they focus on doing or changing something, they have a reasonable probability of being successful. This can be very powerful in choosing the "right fork" in the road.

SOME TAKE-AWAYS FOR YOU TO CONSIDER

This chapter has been a bit more complex than the others, and we want to make sure we leave you with some specific take-aways before you move on in your ALD journey. Here are some high points to remember and apply:

- You self-regulate a change in what you do if you are not fully aware of the area that needs to be changed. Self-awareness is the basis for self-regulated development.
- You can go from self-awareness to self-regulation and back again. This can occur as you begin to realize things about yourself while you're experiencing the self-regulated change process. This circular or feedback loop is one of the ways we come to learn more about what constitutes our actual self.
- The more you are vested in a particular way of thinking and/or behaving, the more likely it is that you will go from self-awareness to self-regulation.

- Building in milestones that will help you gauge where you are in the self-regulation process will be key to sustaining the change process over time. The milestones should represent specific levels of accomplishment in order that you reinforce yourself for positive, incremental change.
- The leadership that you work with can be a positive or negative contributor to helping you stay focused on the things you are changing via self-regulation. Trying to self-regulate change against managerial forces that are set against the change is likely to result in failure.
- Self-regulation should probably never occur alone. Having a support system is critical to sustaining success.

Finally, whatever you take away from this chapter, your goal is to take the "right" fork in the road of staying on course or changing. Part of the strategy in ALD involves saying exactly what you mean to other people. So once you commit to do something different, do not deviate—you must stay the new course. Do not waffle; be consistent, and you will build at least conditional trust. Then, over time, you will build trust in you as a person, not in terms of a transaction or contractually. Along the way, the core elements reflected through simple guidelines for authentic leadership that we believe will help you to facilitate any of these changes include the following:

- Stay oriented toward others first, even if it is at your own expense in the short term.
- Remain positive, optimistic, and hopeful in your actions and behaviors.
- Reinforce transparency, so that when you know something is important, others will know, and vice versa.

- Use opportunities where tough decisions were made, such as involving ethical decisions, to debrief and explain the criteria you used to make a decision.
- Encourage others (especially followers) to contribute feedback to enhance your self-awareness so that you minimize any potential blind spots.

We will end this chapter with a real-life story about self-regulation. When Nelson Mandela was in prison on Robben's Island, he came to the realization that he had to engage the white guards in the prison in a dialogue in order to convert them to his way of thinking. Educating them, instead of threatening them to change or simply accepting his seemingly hopeless fate, turned out to be the more powerful option for him and the nation.

To accomplish his objective, Mandela set out to learn the Afrikaans language of the white Afrikaaner, which he did over a several year period. By learning their language, he was able to engage them on their level. This effort on his part, of course, also signaled to them his respect for their culture and traditions. It worked! The guards became some of Mandela's biggest advocates for changing the conditions in the prison. What an amazing impact a little self-regulation can have on a culture, nation, and even an entire continent.

FOR YOU TO DO ON YOUR ALD JOURNEY

We want you to think about the following issues the next time you engage in working with a new group:

1. Consider how you intend to build trust in your leadership and among team members prior to meeting the team. Think about the following points:

- What is the first action you can take to build conditional trust? For example, you could consider delineating your rules of engagement, your red lines, the clear purpose of the team, and your expectations and aspirations, while also finding out what are their red lines, expectations, and aspirations.

- What do you know about each individual? Remember, each individual is unique and will have different expectations about the group's work. Can you commit to spending some individual time with each member to learn about their expectations, what challenges them, how they like to receive recognition, how often they want to receive feedback, and what their concerns are?

- What should your first meeting look like in terms of goals, processes, and intended outcomes? Based on the individual meetings, could you delineate what the mission is, why it's important, the objectives, who owns those objectives, how you work as a leader, getting a start on the rules of engagement, and the milestones you see for gauging achievement?

- Many leaders start teams by focusing on the outcomes versus the process they need in order to be successful and to sustain success over time. We are not suggesting you neglect the outcomes for the team, but that you concentrate on building a "positive team process" that will engage team members from the very start in helping you build what is required for the team to work together and build trust in you and them.

2. One of the organizational requirements that leaders like least is giving formal performance feedback. How can we change the way you give feedback to people you work with so that it becomes a more positive leader and follower experience?

    - Can you identify those areas of follower development and performance that directly affects their performance as both individuals and as a member of a group? If you can, then you can identify the most important areas where feedback should be given to followers.

- What if we set as a maximum that you cannot give feedback on more than three performance domain areas? Following this rule, you can stay very focused on what you are observing in their behavior and performance. With those three areas, you need to set up a simple structure for providing feedback. For example, you may provide three positives to one negative feedback incident as part of the process.

3. Focus on bringing the future to the present. Take a particular area of work and try to focus out into the future and see how that area of work can and should change.

- Set a time span of one to two years to focus on the future.
- Look at people, technology, and business trends two years out.
- Examine how those trends might impact upon your view of the domain you are in, coming up with two alternative views for each trend.
- Talk to people you feel have a strength for focusing on the future. Ask them to articulate what trends they believe will impact the domain you have chosen to focus on.
- Revisit after six months and see if you would change the trend line and to assess how you have progressed so far. Are you ready?

LEADERSHIP NOTES

- *We are all the authors of our own lives.* We can determine the choices we make in terms of the path we go down, but we need to also take the time to reflect on what's most important to us and to those we lead.

- *Many leaders escalate their commitment to a failing cause.* Leaders will often stay the course on a disastrous track, even though all of the signs point to the need for a course correction. This escalation to commitment can be challenged if followers feel reinforced to challenge the basic assumptions of their leaders.

- *To help followers know where to enter and not enter with challenges, leaders need to specify their red zones.* It is incumbent upon the leader to define the criteria for acceptable and unacceptable behavior and performance. Many leaders do not clearly establish what is not acceptable, and thus do not provide followers with the appropriate direction to challenge and to perform.

7

ALD AND PSYCAP

TRADITIONALLY, our business schools and the implicit theories of business leaders have been almost solely based on the perspective of the value of economic and financial capital: how to invest in it and gain a return from it. The vast majority of this education and the resulting practice of capitalism has been concerned with how to raise financial capital, account for it, budget it, leverage it, and impact the "bottom line," also known as: "Show me the money!"

In these tumultuous times, as we have said, with its truncated periods between each set of significantly different times, such economic and financial capital is finally being recognized as not entirely sufficient. Both business schools and at least authentic leaders still recognize the value of financial capital as a necessary foundation for today's and future organizations, but they now also understand that financial and economic capital is not the only considerations impacting upon sustained growth and competitive advantage.

THE EMERGENCE OF HUMAN CAPITAL

The economic term "capital" refers to the resources that are withdrawn from consumption and invested for future anticipated returns. Over the years, such capital has been equated with tangible assets such as money and physical goods such as plant, equipment, inventories, technological processes, data of all kinds, and even intellectual property like patents, copyrights, and trademarks. In recent years, both academics and enlightened business leaders have recognized what Baruch Lev, an accounting professor from NYU, has referred to as the "intangible assets" of organizations. Intel's Andy Grove, for another example, referring to human assets, has said, "Our most important assets walk out the door every night."

Human capital is now seen as vital to the competitive advantage of organizations. Why? Because, unlike money, physical assets, and technology—which can be readily transferable and purchased like a commodity on the open market—human capital is unique. It is made up of education, skills, experience, and tacit knowledge that cannot be imitated or easily duplicated or purchased. If developed properly, human capital can contribute to an enduring, sustainable, and competitive advantage for today's organizations.

NEWLY RECOGNIZED SOCIAL CAPITAL

Recently, both academic and, to a degree, real-world discussions have even gone beyond human capital by proposing the added value of "social capital." Where traditional economic/financial capital can be simply defined as "what you have," and human capital is "what you know," social capital is "who you know." More precisely, social capital is made up of relationships and the network of contacts and friends that can facilitate getting done what you need to accomplish.

Extensive Gallup research over the years has clearly found that friendship networks lead to more engaged employees and higher performance. As Gallup practice leader Curt Coffman notes: "Great managers understand this, and they encourage their employees to develop strong networks that support and encourage them. And the degree of trust that exists in those relationships will determine how employees get through difficult times." As an intangible capital asset, it is the value of these social relationships, and the value of the networks in which people are included and develop over time—based on trust and understanding each other—that provides this newly recognized social capital.

Human capital can be fairly, objectively estimated based on criteria such as years of education and experience, and the expertise and qualifications people possess for completing the mission and critical tasks. Social capital can also be calculated based on network analysis and the quality of these relationships that exist in the organization. Such measures of social capital would include mutual trust, transparency, support, openness, and so on.

Objective judgments can be made on how relationships help support the exchange of information, acceptance, knowledge, and expertise. In organizations where there are excellent social relationships and transparency levels are high, we can expect there will be a relatively high level of social capital.

Potentially equal to, if not exceeding, the value of economic/financial and human capital, social capital can take a tremendous amount of work to build, bank, and utilize effectively. For instance, simply losing one or two key individuals from a social network, or the loss of trust over even one incident, can rapidly draw down the social capital bank account to critical levels. Now imagine what happens when two companies merge in a hostile environment. What impact do you think such a hostile "marriage" will have on the level of social capital in the new organization?

Unlike human capital, in some ways social capital acts like financial capital since a network of colleagues (like money) can be used in many ways—for information gathering, building constituency commitment to a particular mission, or to connect expert sources for required information and knowledge. And like any other form of development, social capital needs to be nurtured to enhance its value over time. In particular, the top leadership of an organization can have a significant impact on creating the appropriate conditions for sharing knowledge capital.

As an example of identifying and building social capital, Gallup's Coffman suggests: "First, managers should encourage employees to name their best friends at work and help them think of ways to nourish those relationships. Second, they can encourage employees to think about the people in their lives—inside and outside the company—who help them grow and develop."

In addition to such practical guidelines, we propose that ALD can be one of the key drivers in the development of social capital. By creating transparency and trust in relationships, for instance, authentic leaders are building the base for social networks. Such networks based on trust will be more alive with rich information and knowledge that is accurate, useful, and available. We expect that the authentic leader is a central part of the social network, at a minimum creating the conditions for social networks to blossom.

Social capital represents the conduit for great ideas in organizations and can be fueled by authentic leadership development.

THE BACKGROUND AND FACTORS OF PSYCAP

So far we have merely made you aware or reacquainted you with the terms and basic meaning of human and social capital. As part of ALD, we feel these newly emerging forms of capital can contribute considerable value and competitive advantage to today's organizations and, perhaps more important, to those emerging and readying themselves to compete over the next 25 years. However, in accordance with our theme throughout of presenting truly cutting edge, "out of the box" thinking and concepts on ALD, we want to go beyond human and social capital and bring you what we call positive psychological capital, or simply PsyCap.

We define PsyCap as going beyond human (what you know) and social (who you know) capital to "who you are" (the actual self) and "what you intend to become" (your possible self). Drawing from our discussion in earlier chapters, and applying it to the ALD process, PsyCap involves investing in the actual self to reap the return of becoming the possible self. At least for ALD, we cannot think of a better and potentially more productive use of the concept of capital than this PsyCap.

Though our work with Gallup, we were able to get in on the ground floor of the positive psychology movement. The field of positive psychology was initiated by well-known researcher Martin Seligman in his role as president of the American Psychological Association in 1998. He and a few other colleagues felt that psychology had become too preoccupied with a disease model and mental illness. They proactively jump-started positive psychology by emphasizing what is right with people, rather than just what is wrong. Positive psychologists value the strengths and virtues of people, rather than weakness and dysfunction.

The positive, strength-based approach was in line with Gallup's consulting practice and corporate values, and it led them to sponsor the first and subsequent annual Positive Psychology summits. Fred's early participation in these summits inspired him to apply positive psychology concepts to the workplace, which later dovetailed with Bruce's work on transformational leadership, given its positive focus on developing followers to their full potential.

Fred wrote some initial articles a few years ago defining what he called positive organizational behavior (POB) as:

1. Positive and unique,
2. Based on theory, research, and valid measures

3. Open to development and change (or statelike as opposed to fixed, traitlike)
4. Manageable for performance improvement

These scientific criteria differentiate POB from the popular positive literature or motivational speakers and armchair gurus (like "Who Moved My Cheese" or Tony Robbins), which are not based on theory or research, have no valid measures, and have not systematically demonstrated impact on performance. These POB criteria also differentiate from positive psychology itself, which is mostly concerned with more trait-like, or relatively fixed, character virtues, and thus not open to development, and are also not directly concerned with performance or the workplace.

Over the years, the field of organizational behavior has recognized positive concepts (e.g., positive affectivity or positive reinforcement), and as our colleague Bernie Bass has noted: "Positive psychology was being applied in organizational psychology long before it took root in clinical psychology. It was observed as better management but not explained theoretically." However, like psychology, we would argue that such positive concepts have not been given enough attention, and that there is indeed a need for more theory-building, better understanding, and guided research for effective applications.

Recently, a group of organizational scholars at the University of Michigan revealed, a complementary approach to POB that they call "positive organizational scholarship" (POS). The major difference between this POS and POB is that POS tends to be more macro-oriented and does not meet the POB criteria of being statelike and thus open for development and directly concerned with performance impact. POS is concerned with what is extremely positive—what they call "positive deviance"—in organizations, such as high degrees of compassion, forgiveness, gratitude, and virtuousness. Together, the two approaches can be used to present a more positive framework in which to examine ALD.

To take off from the idea of human and social capital, we have used POB as the theoretical roots and point of departure for what we call "positive psychological capital," or PsyCap. Fred and colleagues wrote the original articles on PsyCap a couple of years ago (they can be found in issues of *Business Horizons* and *Organizational Dynamics* published in 2004), and they define it as a core factor consisting of criteria meeting POB states such as, but not limited to, self-efficacy/confidence, hope, optimism, and resiliency. Our chapter on "Authentic Leadership" in the *Positive Organizational Scholarship* book uses PsyCap as both an important antecedent and input role in ALD (the actual self) as well as an outcome (the possible self, that is not only transparent, moral/ethical, future-oriented, and associate building, but also confident, hopeful, optimistic, and resilient).

The remainder of this chapter drills down a bit on the major components of PsyCap and how they relate to ALD. It should be noted that self-efficacy, or confidence, may best meet our established criteria for PsyCap, but since we gave it considerable coverage in Chapters 4 and 6, we will concentrate here on hope, optimism, and resiliency. The next chapter will focus on how PsyCap can be developed in oneself and others as part of the ALD process.

PSYCAP HOPE

Hope is a commonly used, everyday term. However, as a criteria-meeting dimension of PsyCap, hope is defined by positive psychologist Rick Snyder as constituting what he calls the "will" and the "way." Specifically, Snyder and his colleagues precisely define hope as a positive motivational state that is based on an interactively derived sense of successful agency or goal-directed energy(willpower), and pathways or planning to meet goals (way power).

Willpower represents a strong belief and sense of confidence that one will succeed, and is more internalized than way power, which represents what Snyder calls "pathways thinking." It is this pathways component that mainly differentiates hope from optimism, confidence, and other PsyCap factors. This pathways thinking also fits well with ALD. Authentic leaders are constantly generating appropriate alternatives in order to attain desired goals, objectives, and the overall mission.

At the core of pathways thinking is the reference to time and how a person will get from the "present" (the actual self) to the "future" (possible self). High-hope individuals will look for different ways to bring the future to the present. When high hopers are confronted with obstacles, they will seek different pathways for pursuing the future goal, mission, and vision.

As an example, when faced with a slumping economy, the head of a sales unit that has decreasing revenues may address the team by saying something like: "We cannot do anything about the economy, but I know we can get through our current problems. I am proposing two feasible alternatives that we can employ to get our numbers back on track." This hopeful leader has both the willpower ("I know we can get through this") and way power ("I am proposing two feasible alternatives") to accomplish the goal, mission, and vision of the unit.

In their considerable research stream, Snyder and his colleagues have found that high-hope individuals will develop a plan they believe has a high probability of success. Significantly, however, high-hope individuals also make sure they have alternative, contingency plans in place in case the original one does not work. For the low-hope individual, pathway thinking is more limited and alternative paths are not well-established. Those with low hope tend to be more reactive.

Drawing from positive psychologist Barbara Fredrickson's work, which we cited earlier in the book, we would expect that high-hope leaders, as part of their ALD process, will seek, in her words, to "broaden and build" their followers to be more positive about future prospects. In terms of PsyCap hope, high-hope leaders will have greater willpower and way power to successfully take on challenges. Through personal example, high hopers will build the PsyCap of those around them. This building of hope enables everyone to be more successful.

In initial research with our colleagues we have found that managers with higher levels of measured hope are rated as better performers and are more satisfied with and committed to their organizations. In addition, the higher the managers' hope, the correspondingly higher their work units' financial performance, as well as better retention and greater satisfaction among their employees. We have also found a positive link between entrepreneurs' hope levels and their satisfaction with business ownership. We even found that with a large sample of Chinese factory workers undergoing dramatic economic and social transformational changes, the higher their measured hope, the higher their performance is rated.

In research directly related to ALD, we found that the higher the hope levels of followers, the more authentic they viewed their leaders to be. The beauty of these research findings is that since hope can be a state, rather than just a fixed trait, it can be developed in both leaders and followers, with resulting positive performance outcomes. Leaders can propagate hope and create the conditions for it to flourish in organizations.

Many traditional leaders may have the will to succeed or deep beliefs and convictions, but they have lost the way. According to Snyder, this would reduce the level of overall hope and reduce its positive impact. By the same token, knowing the way to succeed or establishing the pathway, but not having the belief or the will, can also reduce the level of hope and limit its impact. To draw from this hope dimension of PsyCap, authentic leaders need both the willpower and way power.

Throughout the moments that one accumulates in life, the positive moments that matter will especially build both the will and way, and therefore increase one's hope. Unfortunately, there are other moments that can drain both dimensions of hope. ALD needs to make sure that enough moments transpire with leaders and their followers to build sufficient will power and way power to sustain performance, even when faced with the most intractable of problems and inevitable obstacles.

Your psychological capital can be boosted by the positive moments you are fortunate enough to have provided and to create.

We have all been in organizations where leaders and followers have what appears to be a campaign to drain hope, every drop of it. They often do so by blaming others for the areas of responsibility they can control. Being in control is one of the determinants of hope.

For example, what has become known as the "Powell Doctrine" relates to the military (and by extension it's now applied to the geopolitical realm as well) always knowing clearly the mission, milestones, and exit strategy. We have seen when we are uncertain of the mission, not sure of the milestones, and unaware of the potential exit strategy, that one's hope as a belief and a way are severely drained.

There are many traditional leaders who believe and hope that they and their followers and organizations will improve effectiveness and performance over the next time period. This hope stems from a belief in themselves and those they work with in the organization. Such beliefs can become collective and therefore contagiously positive.

To enhance levels of hope and have its desired effects, from a PsyCap perspective, we must also consider how the pathway challenges are being addressed. Put in other terms, we may believe in our mission and strategy, but we also must have alternative implementation methods in place to be successful. Knowing the way (alternatives for implementation and contingency plans) provides an increase in the level of hope.

ALD builds the belief in what can be accomplished by self and followers, and also points to the way that it can be accomplished.

ALD can develop and enhance hope by building into leaders the beliefs and the ways that those beliefs can be actualized.

There is almost always at least one pathway someone didn't consider. In that one pathway, there is increased hope that can result in desired outcomes. Also, since ALD builds trust in followers, it allows the leader a little more time to get to where he or she feels they need to be, and that too reinforces hope.

PSYCAP OPTIMISM

Like hope, optimism is a commonly used word. It is used in everyday language to describe those who exude a positive sense of what can be accomplished. However, more precisely, positive psychology treats optimism as expecting a positive outcome.

Research has shown that optimists interpret both successes and failures differently than pessimists. Optimists, for instance, do not take failures as personally (it's not their fault). They view failure as only a temporary setback and only in this situation. On the other hand, pessimists make the opposite attributions—they take failures personally, as long lasting, and generalize to everything they do.

When optimists fail, or when they have a setback or encounter a problem, it does not draw down a positive sense of themselves nor shatter their self-awareness. Although optimists are commonly portrayed as naive and quickly disappointed when things don't go their way, recent basic research finds the opposite.

Award-winning positive psychologist Suzanne Segerstrom found that optimists are "wiser in expending their energies and better at directing their attention to and elaborating on positive information." Their optimism coincides with a considerable source of positive energy and effectiveness that can become contagious.

Optimism stems from the probability one associates with a general direction to be pursued and would not necessarily be as specific as what we have described with respect to self-efficacy (covered in Chapters 4 and 6) or hope. Taking our earlier example of the leader faced with a declining economy, she can be optimistic that things will turn around this year. However, if we're working for her, this may not necessarily increase our self-efficacy/confidence that our unit will achieve its specific goals, nor will it increase our hope by providing an alternative pathway.

Our self-efficacy is based more on what we can or cannot do, and our hope on willpower and contingency pathways. Optimism, it should be noted, may stimulate and provide a higher base for setting your level of confidence and kick into action (triggering hope) your willpower and some alternative ways to accomplish the goals. In other words, the various PsyCap states are interactive with one another, though considerable theory and research clearly indicates these PsyCap states are different and independent from one another.

Optimism may vary as a function of how much confidence and trust you have in your leader, your fellow employees, your organization's strengths, and what is happening outside, with family, community, or country. Like the other PsyCap factors, optimism is a state that is affected by what is happening around us, and often what just happened. Optimism is something that can be changed with recognition from one's leader that "Everything will be okay, we'll make it, and all is on track for success."

In one of the most widely recognized work-related studies involving PsyCap states, the founding father of positive psychology, Martin Seligman, found in one of his early studies that optimistic sales agents at Metropolitan Life Insurance sold significantly more than the sales agents who had less measured optimism. He also discovered that the more optimistic sales agents had better retention rates, which are vitally important in the insurance industry. Considerable related research has also confirmed the connections between optimism and higher levels of performance at work, school, and on the athletic field.

Our own preliminary research with colleagues has found a strong relationship between leader and associate optimism and their rated performance and work-related attitudes such as satisfaction and commitment. For example, a study in a large hospital found a strong correlation between the nurses' level of optimism and their rated overall performance and customer/patient satisfaction. Can you even imagine the impact that a negative nurse would have on patients? Unfortunately, there are such negative, pessimistic nurses out there, but the optimistic ones are evaluated by supervisors and patients as being more effective.

Some recent evidence is emerging from Gallup's research that just a small dose of optimism from a nurse or doctor can result in shorter hospital stays, quicker recovery, and obviously less cost to our healthcare system. Similar to hope, we also found followers' optimism was positively related to their view of the authenticity of their leaders. So, once again, developing the PsyCap factor of optimism in oneself and in followers does indeed seem to facilitate the ALD process, just as the ALD process can create the conditions for higher PsyCap.

Components of PsyCap can have a profound, positive, physical and psychological impact.

PSYCAP RESILIENCY

In positive psychology, resiliency represents patterns of positive adaptation in the context of significant adversity or risk. In simple terms it is the "bounce back" we see in people who have experienced a problem or even failure.

The PsyCap factor of resiliency is exhibited by those who are hit hard by a particular problem or challenge but still find some way to keep moving ahead. Resilient people bounce back and even beyond, never bemoaning the past or the present.

Think back to what happened to you the day after you received the bad news that you failed at something important to you, perhaps a rejection of a proposed business initiative. How long did it take you to recover and to return to a place where you were positive about the prospects of moving forward? What were your thoughts right after learning about the rejection—the very first thoughts? These are all indications of what constitutes your capacity for resiliency.

A recent *Harvard Business Review* article by Diane Coutu summarized the considerable theory and research on resiliency from clinical psychology, as it relates to business leadership, as "a staunch acceptance of reality; a deep belief, often buttressed by strongly held values, that life is meaningful; and an uncanny ability to improvise." In other words, these components of PsyCap resiliency are compatible with and even embedded within the ALD process presented in this book. Unquestioning self-awareness, belief in oneself and the mission, and the ability to adapt over time, are all part of the authentic leader's psychological capital of resiliency.

In terms of dealing with negative moments in the ALD life course, recent American Psychological Association president Robert Sternberg notes: "What we do not realize when we are younger is that almost all of us go through these periods of staggering defeat or, at least, uncertainty. The question is not whether you will go through it; it is how you will come out of it."

Those who are able to draw from their PsyCap reservoir of resiliency in bouncing back and beyond from the negative but inevitable moments that matter are on their way to ALD. As Sternberg concludes, "What distinguishes those who are highly successful from others is, in large part, resilience in the face of humiliation, defeats, and setbacks of various kinds."

In a landmark study on resiliency in the workplace, noted psychologist Salvatore Maddi studied 13,000 employees who had been downsized in one year from Illinois Bell Telephone. As is too often the case, the IBT downsizing decision created enormous anxiety and adversity for most employees. In fact, Maddi found that two-thirds of the employees suffered significant performance and health declines as a result of the downsizing. Noteworthy, however, he found the remaining third actually thrived during the upheaval, despite the same disruption and stress. These resilient employees maintained their health, happiness, and performance, and many even experienced renewed enthusiasm. Developing this PsyCap of resiliency and leveraging it in the turbulent times facing most organizations today would seem to be a very wise investment.

Our own initial research with colleagues verifies what Maddi discovered. Like the other PsyCap factors, we have found significant relationships between leaders' and associates' level of measured resiliency and their performance and work attitudes. In fact, in our study of the Chinese workers mentioned earlier, we found that their resiliency related relatively stronger to performance than the other PsyCap factors of hope and optimism. This makes sense because the sample included state-owned and privately owned factories, both of which were undergoing dramatic transitions in the new China (WTO, competitive pressures, downsizing, and changing expectations and lifestyles).

Finally, in another study, the followers' level of resiliency, like the other PsyCap states, related to the perception of their leader's authenticity. These findings again demonstrate the potential value of developing resiliency PsyCap in oneself and in followers in the ALD process.

HOW MUCH IS IN YOUR PSYCAP BANK?

Like most things involving human beings, it's what you do well beforehand that leverages into benefits downstream. You might at this point start by asking yourself where your PsyCap bank account stands today. How much confidence, hope, optimism, and resiliency have shown up in your account?

How much do you regularly contribute to your account, and how much do others—including those whom you lead and those who lead you—contribute to it? How about your contribution to other's accounts as you look to future challenges that will no doubt tap these accounts? Have you planned your PsyCap development in order to build your bank account for a "rainy day" when future challenges will drain some of your PsyCap?

You have to look pretty far downstream to keep in mind that your PsyCap always needs some replenishment and augmentation.

Wouldn't it be interesting to get each and every leader out there thinking about their contribution to each follower's and fellow leader's PsyCap account? As Colleen Barrett, president of Southwest Airlines, recently related in a *Harvard Business Review* interview:

> The other day, I was talking to one of our officers, and he said, "How do you do that?" and I said, "How do I do what?" He was referring to a meeting we'd both been at earlier. I'd asked one of the presenters at the meeting, a fellow who reported to this officer, if he was feeling OK. The officer thought the employee was fine, but, it turned out, the poor guy had had a pretty traumatic experience in his personal life the night before. His presentation went well, but he seemed off to me, distracted. I suppose in order to have seen that, I must have been fairly attuned to what this fellow's presentations were usually like.

This leader, in this moment, contributed greatly to this follower's and her fellow leader's PsyCap accounts. Barrett went on to say that she herself gains what we could call her PsyCap from those around her. She admits to getting carried away once in awhile, but "I've learned to rely on calmer people around me to give me those raised eyebrows that say, 'Lower the passion a little bit, and people will listen more.'"

Just like dynamic leader Colleen Barrett, each day you can draw from your own and others' PsyCap accounts, or you can add to them. This is analogous to the recent Gallup best-seller entitled *How Full Is Your Bucket?* by our recently deceased friend and mentor Don Clifton and his grandson, Tom Rath.

In their book, they discuss how people can dip into your bucket each day and drain your energy with cynicism, criticism, and reproof. Or you can go through your day having people add to your positive energy bucket through recognition, respect, and support.

The balance in this metaphorical energy bucket is similar to the one in a PsyCap bank account. However, we are focusing more specifically on the components of PsyCap, while Tom and Don's approach is broader and more inclusive of positive emotions and simple recognition.

As the major theme in our book suggests, "every moment matters"—in this case to building up our PsyCap accounts. ALD requires PsyCap investment, but the short- and especially the long-term return is a winner for self, followers, and the organization. Paul Stoltz, in a *Leader to Leader* article, cites the role moments play in PsyCap in the following example.

Odwalla, a successful health food producer, had a terrible moment occur when a number of people came down with E.coli after drinking the firm's popular unpasteurized apple-based juices. The reaction of customers and the media to the company was swift and deadly: Sales plunged 90 percent overnight and the firm lost millions in product recalls and lawsuits. They could have closed up and never been heard from again. Instead, as Stoltz related, "something deep inside the men and women who led the company—and within the many other dedicated members of the Odwalla team—refused to let that happen."

We would say the Odwalla team drew their confidence, hope, optimism, and especially their resiliency from their PsyCap account. They must have had a lot to draw on because they came back from this brink of disaster stronger than ever. They tripled their sales and built the best product safety and testing program in the industry.

Like the Odwalla leaders, you can open and develop this PsyCap account at any time in your life stream and ALD process. "Hopefully" this will happen in time for when you need it.

THE ROLE OF SELF-AWARENESS IN PSYCAP

Let's start with a basic premise we have been drawing upon throughout this book. You must first be aware of your own PsyCap (your actual self) in order to have a profoundly positive impact on developing and building your own and others PsyCap. Such self-awareness is increasingly recognized by authentic leaders.

An example would be Andrea Jung, chair and CEO of Avon Products, who recently noted in a *Harvard Business Review* interview: "Of all a leader's competencies, emotional and otherwise, self-awareness is the most important. Without it, you can't identify the impact you have on others. Self-awareness is very important for me as CEO." So we now return to the concept of self-awareness and then self-regulation as it relates to PsyCap and ALD.

Regarding levels of self-awareness, when have you given any specific consideration to your levels of confidence, hope, optimism, and resiliency? Try to think back to a time that was essentially a nonevent where you thought about how optimistic you were about something coming true. We use a nonevent here because we're sure that people typically think about how optimistic they were following negative events, challenges, and failures.

Often, we find that most people think in terms of disturbing moments; how they can recover and get back to where they were prior to a setback or failure. Although we consider such thinking important, it is a limited way of building your own PsyCap and the PsyCap of those around you.

If you only consider your PsyCap in moments of failure or duress, you're not maximizing the potential of PsyCap. In fact, you may be falling prey to what clinical psychologists call a "deficits reduction model." This psychodynamic model comes to the forefront when we have experienced a setback and then look for a course correction to rebalance our position or equilibrium.

What we have found is that there is much more in the PsyCap account than just simply rebalancing it. However, this does assume you keep it foremost in your self-awareness and add to it perhaps when it is least needed in the many moments that occur each day.

One way to go beyond merely rebalancing and maintaining an equilibrium is to constantly seek honest feedback from others. Avon's Jung does this with a trusted, open CEO advisory counsel and, interestingly, her own kids. She has the following to say about these two trusted sources of feedback. Her advisory counsel, representing the whole company across the world, tells her

> . . . the good, the bad, and the ugly about the company. Anything can be said. It helps keep me connected to what people really think and how my actions affect them. I also rely on my children for honest appraisals. You can get a huge dose of reality by seeing yourself through your children's eyes, noticing the ways they react to and reflect what you say and do. My kids are part of my 360-degree feedback. They're the most honest of all.

So, good old honest feedback contributing to greater self-awareness is one way to develop and build PsyCap. In the next chapter we turn to some other, more "out of the box" ways to also build out your own and others' PsyCap that are especially relevant to your ALD process.

SOME TAKE-AWAYS FOR YOU TO CONSIDER

The main purpose of this chapter was to introduce you to the core concepts of a psychological strength index that we have labeled your positive psychological capital, or PsyCap. One of our core messages is that you must be aware of the investments that can be made in this PsyCap and its growth in order to track the overall development and potential of your organization. Measuring and tracking this psychological capital is in our view as critical as all other capital metrics (economic/financial, human, and social), even though it has almost been totally ignored in the past.

Some other essential take aways for your ALD development and the development of others includes the following:

- It is important to break hope down into the will and the way when considering how to boost it in yourself and others.
- Moments that you create and take advantage of can enhance your optimism. Having an authentic track record can be leveraged to build optimism through the trust others place in your leadership over time. When you are optimistic, it appears authentic.
- We have asked you to consider how you bounce back from difficult experiences and the support you provide for others. Resiliency is an essential ingredient in the core PsyCap concept and measures.
- PsyCap is not only about the individual psychological states and human capital, but also the social networks that create connections between individuals. This social capital can also

enhance PsyCap levels. Like PsyCap, effective social networks are largely determined by authentic leadership.

FOR YOU TO DO ON YOUR ALD JOURNEY

We would like you to do a little human accounting exercise with yourself and your closest peers and followers. First, take each of the PsyCap components and on a scale from 0 to 100, judge your present level of confidence, hope, optimism, and resiliency, with 0 being the lowest and 100 tops. Ask your colleagues to do the same on their own.

Next, identify events or moments on the left-hand side of a page that have been positive, raising your bank account of PsyCap to whatever level it is currently. Do the same on the right-hand side for events or moments that have drawn down your PsyCap bank account. Ask your colleagues to complete the same exercise.

Now one final step: Identify those moments or events you could have controlled and those you had no control over, at least before you became aware of the event. If you had control over them, what could you have done to enhance the positives and minimize the negatives? If you had no control, then what could you have done at the time you realized the "moment" in terms of regaining confidence, hope, optimism, and resiliency?

Get together with your colleagues to see how each of you has rated your PsyCap and completed your respective analyses of moments. You may see some variations in PsyCap that are not due to the situation at work. There may be things occurring outside of work that naturally bleed over into work and drain your PsyCap.

Now discuss one action you can take collectively to reinforce and grow PsyCap. Take only one that you can commit to doing over the next month. Commit to your own action as well as one that can reinforce your PsyCap, ideally reinforcing your group's action. The action should be as simple as possible. For example, end all meetings discussing what worked after critiquing what didn't, or never leave a strategy session without at least two additional paths to pursue if the first one fails.

LEADERSHIP NOTES

- Leaders must focus on growing their own psychological capital, because its growth will impact the PsyCap of followers as well as the social capital of the organization. To grow one's PsyCap requires attention to self-awareness. This can be derived from positive experiences, while at the same time creating positive moments to replenish one's PsyCap account.

- There is a revolution occurring today, where we are now discovering the enormous benefits from focusing on strengths first versus weaknesses, and complementing that focus by escalating the number of positive moments. We have gone from a pop psychology view of being positive to one where basic and applied science is showing the enormous benefits to creating a positive individual, group, and work climate. We call this psychological capital, or PsyCap.

- The interaction of PsyCap components such as confidence, hope, optimism, and resiliency produces a greater impact on work performance, and attitudes than any one of these positive states by themselves. In PsyCap, the whole is greater than the sum of its parts. There is a synergistic effect from PsyCap on the ALD process.

8

BUILDING OUT PSYCAP

NOW THAT YOU HAVE a good grasp of the foundation and meaning of PsyCap and how it relates to the ALD process, this chapter turns to how you develop, "build-out," your own Psy-Cap and that of others.

Let's look at your PsyCap account in a somewhat different way than we did in the last chapter. Let's assume that you could revalidate your levels of PsyCap every day. This may seem far-fetched, but consider the Gallup Organization as an example.

As we have said, the Gallup Organization has built its consulting business and brand on what it calls a "strength-based approach" to human development. They believe that a positive human condition is a prerequisite for achieving sustainable growth and exemplary performance. They configure their consulting services around identifying people's strengths and then focus on building the strengths of the entire organization.

In contrast to the deficits reduction model in clinical psychology, Gallup's approach is actually "antideficit." Like the positive psychology movement, the company strives to focus their interventions on reinforcing what's right with people versus the deficits or what's wrong. Practicing what they preach, when Gallup associates log onto their e-mail each day, they're asked to complete one question that taps into the degree of positive energy they feel. The premise is that this positive energy translates into positive action, and positive action in turn translates into positive organizational growth and performance.

Several days after the 9/11 terrorist attack on the World Trade Center, Bruce was with Gallup CEO Jim Clifton while he was reviewing data on that premise for the New York office. Jim was pinpointing the significant drop in this office's overall level of positivity based on trend data and comparisons to other Gallup locations around the world. His concerns were based in part on how his employees were doing emotionally following the traumatic event. But that was not his sole basis of concern.

Clifton believes, and continually advocates, that positive energy is a force multiplier, and that it leads to a competitive advantage in terms of business development and growth. As the CEO of Gallup, the precipitous drop in positive energy in the New York office staff's performance would of course concern him. Indeed, this single item might be an important leading indicator of a drop-off in future business growth.

By tracking the state of positive energy each day, as measured in the e-mail question noted above—a global metric of sorts related to PsyCap—Clifton was reaffirming its importance in terms of maintaining and growing Gallup's consulting practices. Significantly, at the same time he was also showing deep concern for the well-being of his Gallup associates.

The engagement linkages made by Gallup are quite simple. The more positive associates are about their work, the more they are engaged with their organization, and thus the more effort they put forth and work they do. We can take this further, since the more engaged they are in their work, the more they will engage with customers, which results in loyal customers, organic business growth, and ultimately profit and value for the organization. Gallup calls these engagement linkages the "Gallup Path," and it serves as an effective blueprint for their consulting business.

Tracking the level of positivity over time allows leaders to know when events are bringing the PsyCap of their followers down, suggesting it's time for action.

BACK TO SELF-AWARENESS

Let's focus more directly than we did in the last chapter on the role self-awareness has in PsyCap and the ALD process. Recently, David Gergen, well-known TV commentator, advisor to several U.S. Presidents, and a professor in Harvard's Kennedy School of Government, noted in an interview in *Harvard Business Review* that throughout American history leaders have had to better understand themselves and become more self-aware before they could become effective.

Gergen's observation can be readily seen with George Washington, who became more self-aware of his fiery temper and then regulated it. Abraham Lincoln's awareness and then control of his deep melancholia is another example. And it can be seen in FDR's carefree lifestyle, struck down by polio at age 39, his keen self-awareness transforming him into a strong wartime leader and also a more empathetic, caring, domestic leader.

In addition to these examples of self-awareness and how it contributed to the PsyCap and ALD of these historically prominent presidential leaders, Gergen also cites the contemporary examples of Richard Nixon and Bill Clinton. These two Presidents made progress in their self-awareness, but eventually paid a stiff price for not quite getting there.

In our terms, at the end of his presidency, Nixon was not able to reach into his reserve—his PsyCap bank account. His tank was empty when he resigned, largely because of his lack of self-awareness. Clinton, on the other hand, did seem to have some PsyCap left in his tank, and despite some health problems, remains to this day confident, hopeful, optimistic, and resilient.

There are lessons to be learned from these high profile leaders and their struggles with self-awareness and the impact of their PsyCap on their ALD. One such lesson can be summarized by Gergen's observation that "what we have been told since the time of the Greeks is that every leader must try to control his own passions before he can hope to command the passions of others."

Again, we return to the question of the last time you thought about your own self-awareness in relation to your PsyCap of confidence, hope, optimism, or resiliency. Was it when we asked you to do the exercise at the end of the last chapter? What were the conditions impinging upon you at that time?

By thinking about your PsyCap states, we're asking you to do what we might call "self-validation." In large part, only you can determine what your PsyCap level is. This is true even though people around you are making that judgment about you.

Positively control your own passions to positively control others.

You may be quite self-aware of your PsyCap, but unless your behavior actually demonstrates acts of confidence, hopeful statements (both the will and the way), realistic optimism, and the ability to bounce back from setbacks, others may simply view you as self-absorbed. In fact, some social psychologists, such as John Mayer—who, along with Peter Salovey, is credited with a lot of the seminal work on emotional intelligence—feel that too much self-awareness may actually lead to a reduction of self-esteem.

We would argue that self-esteem is more traitlike, or relatively fixed. Thus, it tends to be resistant to change, even through more self-awareness. However, we do need to acknowledge there may potentially be a downside to self-awareness—if it leads to self-absorption.

Despite this possibility, however, self-awareness remains a vital part of the ALD process. People around you will describe your PsyCap states specifically based on what you do following significant moments. Your PsyCap will also be determined by what you do as a pattern of behavior over time.

Surely, after meeting someone, even for just a short time, you've heard people discuss how confident, hopeful, or optimistic they appeared to be. Also, we all marvel at how resilient some leaders are. Take the recently deceased Yasir Arafat. Regardless of the emotional controversy surrounding him, for 40 years he was synonymous with the Palestinian people's persistence to establish their own country.

While Bruce was in Beijing at the time of Arafat's death, a human interest story appeared in the *China Daily* in which a Chinese government leader recalled a story about Mr. Arafat when bad weather forced his plane to be grounded in China several years before. He remembered Arafat becoming upset about not being able to leave for another meeting outside China and telling officials that he would abide by their request to keep his plane grounded if the mayor of the city would spend the night talking with him about China, politics, and world events. The mayor agreed to meet with Arafat, and throughout the night and into the next day the mayor noted how confident Arafat seemed to be. The Palestinian leader regaled him with his optimism and hope for his people, and the mayor marveled at how proud Arafat was of his own and his people's resiliency to come back from setback after setback.

Arafat was indeed relentless in pursuit of his cause, whatever the rest of the world thought about him. Each day, he worked to achieve his goal, even when grounded by the weather or hunkered down in a besieged compound, as he was during the last two years of his life.

The Chinese official said that Arafat's staff repeatedly tried to get him to take a few hours rest. But Arafat felt there was no time to rest, only knew he had to keep moving forward one step at a time. He had, and outwardly exhibited to his followers and the world, considerable PsyCap to the end.

BUILDING PSYCAP THROUGH SELF-AWARENESS: ONE MORE TIME

As you know by now, we believe ALD requires an incredible amount of self-awareness. However, this comes off as a cliché, even to us. So let's be more specific about what we mean by building your PsyCap through self-awareness.

First, you need to be aware of what to track in order to become more self-aware. Our earlier example of Gallup's Jim Clifton tracking positive energy in his company represents such discipline in contributing to and outwardly expressing his self-awareness.

We advocate that a leader is better off just picking one or two things to track or focus on. It should be central to the organization's core organizing principles and values.

As we have said, the core organizing principle and value underlying all of Gallup's internal and business applications is the focus on positivity and strengths. In tracking the positive energy of each associate every day, Clifton outwardly reflects a leader's self-awareness and reinforces his firm's core values.

Second, for PsyCap self-awareness in ALD, you need to build discipline around tracking the intangibles of psychological capital for yourself and your associates. These PsyCap intangibles should be tracked just like most business leaders obsess over all the other metrics regarding their financial and physical capital.

We would argue that tracking the intangibles such as PsyCap will provide you with some leading economic and performance indicators (maybe even better than inventories and financial data). They can help determine where one's business is heading before it actually gets there in the future—bringing, as we have said, the future to the present.

We've found that the mere act of being aware of one's PsyCap in and of itself helps to enhance these psychological strengths over time. Keep in mind that people find it much easier to remember and tend to focus on what went wrong versus what went right.

A prevention focus has been wired into all of us to avoid repeating a bad thing from happening again. But solely focusing on prevention takes away from positivity and can depress levels of confidence, hope, optimism, and resiliency. Since we cannot rewire people to any great extent, for your ALD we advocate adding some new wires of self-awareness of your PsyCap to the mix.

Let's take optimism as an example. Following up on our request at the end of the last chapter, take a look at what you are doing at work right now, and examine your level of optimism on a scale from 0 to 100. What elements of your current work contribute to your level of optimism? Are you missing and/or ignoring anything? Does your optimism include your coworkers? Does it include progress you're making? Does it include any tangible resources you have garnered to be successful? How about your awareness of opportunities that others seem not to be aware of or acting upon at present?

It may be easier to come up with the list of things that are wrong versus right, so putting energy into creating the "right list" is a step toward enhancing your positivity and PsyCap. As well-known organization scientist Karl Weick has said, "If organizing is vulnerable, then positivity tends to be expressed in acts that contain and repair that vulnerability as well as in acts that transcend that vulnerability."

As a leader, and as part of the ALD process, by enhancing your PsyCap you are able to enhance the PsyCap of others around you, and in turn, the overall organization. The opposite, of course, is also true. While you are draining down your own PsyCap, you will also drain others around you, and the organization suffers. Do you recall the bank account analogy we used earlier?

The nature of the human condition is such that the PsyCap accounts of others—especially those who are close to you—will be drawn down or up depending on your level of PsyCap. Indeed, the closer you are to others, the more likely it is that this will occur.

Sometimes you can walk into an organization and immediately feel the level of pessimism and cynicism. These states are not something that naturally comes with an organization's territory.

Negativity is created by the people in an organization, most notably its leaders. These leaders validate negative feelings and behaviors that nearly become hard-wired into, become the culture of, the organization. We say "nearly" hard-wired because there are many instances of a new leader coming into an organization and totally changing the culture. We have often seen this in the movies, but it also occurs with political leaders, and all of us have experienced this at organizational levels.

When President Carter was in his last year of office in 1979, he went on television and gave what has become known as his "malaise speech." In it, he transparently talked about the many problems facing the nation, including the hostages taken by Iranian revolutionaries in Tehran.

The mood of the United States populace at the time of Carter's speech was abysmal, as were his popularity ratings. Then Ronald

Reagan entered the national stage with a "Morning in America" attitude and moving speeches. Whether you liked his policies and politics or not, President Reagan is widely given credit for personally changing the mood of the country in the early 1980s. His persona, if not his charismatic leadership style, changed the mood of people in advance of the supporting economic or sociopolitical data and events.

In the early 1980s the United States was still suffering from inflation, high gas prices, a recession, and nagging problems around the world, although the hostages had been released right after Reagan's inauguration. What Reagan initially brought to the table was a public display of confidence, hope, optimism, and resiliency.

As President, Reagan never wavered, according to associates and knowledgeable observers. Each day, he drew from his considerable PsyCap; he exuded a sense of hope and optimism; he showed resiliency from the Carter years; he was openly confident of what America could accomplish in the down economy and the cold war.

An interesting demonstration of a trigger event also occurred when President Reagan was nearly assassinated by John Hinckley. In those critical moments after being shot, Reagan was still optimistic, demonstrating to the nation that he was in control by what he said to the staff around him. For example, it was widely reported in the media that he said, "Please tell Nancy I am okay, and that I just forgot to duck." And while he was being rolled into surgery, he asked the surgeons whether they were Democrats or Republicans. And then after surgery, literally within days, he was up and going again. He was demonstrating to the world that this oldest U.S. President in history had that bounce-back capacity, his PsyCap of resiliency.

Up to this point we have been discussing what you can specifically do to maintain and build your PsyCap through your sense of self-awareness. To start, you may choose just one PsyCap state to monitor (such as optimism or hope), and then spend several months tracking your credits and debits.

Like the other dimensions of ALD, as we emphasized at the end of the last chapter, focus is a key ingredient in building your PsyCap. This is also true of self-awareness and, ultimately, the accumulation of self-knowledge. Yet, as we have emphasized throughout, ALD never occurs alone.

Authentic leaders are always watched by others, since by definition they stand out from the crowd. So, how others perceived you will impact your PsyCap level, as it did with President Reagan.

The simplest way of putting it is that if your PsyCap drains, it will drain others around you to the extent that they are emotionally connected or engaged with you. Fortunately, in a leadership role, unlike relatively fixed personality traits or character virtues, through your self-awareness you have a choice to contribute and develop your own PsyCap and that of others.

THE WHITE BRIGHT LINE AND THE PYGMALION EFFECT

We can use our analogy, garnered from an interview we discussed in Chapter 2, of the thin white bright line with respect to maintaining and enhancing your own PsyCap and the PsyCap of those around you. The white line of authenticity involves how far one can go in managing the impression one makes upon others regarding levels of confidence, hope, optimism, and resiliency.

We do know that if leaders show confidence that something can get done, it raises this "can do" belief in others. This definitive conclusion comes from a long stream of well-conceived research on the so-called Pygmalion effect that was introduced in an earlier chapter. This term is drawn from mythology of a sculptor/king whose love for a statue brought it to life.

Applying the Pygmalion effect here, research has found that leaders who display a positive belief that challenges what can be achieved in turn increase that belief in others. This seems to hold even when those beliefs may be based on false impressions.

A friend of ours, Israeli organizational psychologist Dov Eden, has clearly demonstrated this Pygmalion effect. He found if leaders believe they are working with effective people, when in fact they are just average, their collective performance is significantly better than a randomly assigned group with comparable actual abilities but whose leader has not told them that they are highly effective. Put another way, if you randomly assign people to two groups and tell the leader that one group is better than the other, when in fact they are not, then the so-called better group will actually perform better. Thus this Pygmalion effect raises the expectations and attainment of success even if based on false data.

It is important to keep in mind that leadership is extremely subtle. In the experiments conducted by Eden, the leaders apparently translated what they were told into their own verbal and nonverbal behavior that cued their followers to higher levels of confidence, hope, and optimism. He and others have discovered that such leaders will also choose to spend more time with those considered to be more capable followers. In so doing, they positively impact their followers' performance.

Ironically, the overwhelming evidence suggests that the leaders in these Pygmalion studies were unaware of their change in behavior. Using the results of these studies as a point of departure, they suggest that you should be more self-aware of your own level of PsyCap. Then, regulating how you exhibit it to others becomes important to the impact you'll have on those around you. Remember, others are always watching and absorbing, even if or when you're not aware of it.

Now, back to the thin white bright line that deals with the gap between what you know and what you want others to know. With respect to follower motivation and performance, if both what you know and want others to know are conscious choices, and are not like the impact of the Pygmalion effect mentioned above, a gray area comes into play. It involves how far leaders can stretch between what they believe is feasible and right and the impressions they want to share with followers. What is the probability of success leaders must have in mind that leads them to believe that desired results are attainable?

Creating the positive myth of Pygmalion or believing so positively that something is going to happen can actually make it happen!

There are some recent troubling research findings from social psychologist David Dunning that "people overestimate themselves, but more than that, they really seem to believe it." In a stream of basic research studies, he discovered that the least competent performers often inflate their abilities the most. Surprisingly, he found that this inflation is mainly due to ignorance, rather than arrogance.

Most applicable to ALD, Dunning also found that self-beliefs, however inaccurate, underlie both subjects' overestimation and underestimation of their competency and how they are doing. These findings certainly throw up a flag of caution when developing the PsyCap of others. However, if anything, the findings reinforce the importance and need for ALD.

Over the years, we have had many interactions with leaders at all levels. Invariably, the most resilient were those who were willing to work with a lower probability of success in conveying to followers their confidence, hope, and optimism that success was attainable. It is the probability that leaders assign and know, and then what they convey through their words and actions, that can demonstrate to others the level of success they believe is attainable.

At one point or another every coach, President, medical practitioner, CEO, teacher, parent, manager, and counselor confronts this dilemma of being realistic but also positive. The line may be crossed where you convey to something slightly beyond, or even a whole lot beyond, what you believe is possible. We do so because the human condition, above all other conditions, is very elastic.

We marvel at those individuals throughout history who appeared to be on the brink of failure but somehow were able to achieve success. Most of our historic, heroic movies (like the recent blockbusters *Troy and Alexander*) have this as the common theme. It starts with the belief that more is possible and the extent to which we believe more in fact is possible, which helps explain the Pygmalion effect noted above.

Remembering the Pygmalion effect or Dunning's research on overestimating competence, how far should you go beyond the probability of success you actually conceive when conveying the probability of success to followers? We believe this question can only be answered by looking to the long term and the trust that followers will have in your judgments about what is and is not feasible in the future.

The judgment one makes as a leader regarding this thin white bright line not only relates to your ALD, it relates to the ALD of those who follow you. Clearly, if the estimates of success that you convey to followers time and again prove wrong, they are likely to lose confidence, hope, optimism, and eventually resiliency. The malaise (remember the Jimmy Carter example) will set in, followed by cynicism and rejection.

Followers are certainly willing to give leaders the benefit of the doubt that failures do occur, even under the most optimistic conditions. So you can be wrong about being successful, but each wrong turn escalates over time. Such gaps are going to reduce their level of PsyCap, as well as your own, and this will have a draining effect on personal and eventually on organizational performance.

FOCUSING ON THE POSITIVE
TO ENHANCE PSYCAP

You have to make your own judgments on how far to reach beyond the available information to portray what you believe constitutes the probability of success. We would suggest that you establish a routine of looking at what positives are working in your favor each day.

Focusing on the positives may actually help you adjust your probability of success and what you convey to others. Nevertheless, from your knowledge about Pygmalion, you must now be sensitive to the fact that how you portray what is possible will have a significant impact on others.

Try to focus on the number of positives that drive effective performance in your organization, and encourage your followers to do the same.

Leaders are the barometers of positivity for followers. They can affect this barometer in many ways. Some leaders recount earlier challenges that have been successfully achieved, thus reminding followers of earlier wins and ways that can enhance subsequent feelings of PsyCap hope.

Even when a group is unsuccessful, by remaining focused they can learn what worked and what didn't work and then come back and improve their performance. Focusing on what went right and wrong can lead to a better and more balanced approach to learning. By learning what is possible to try next, you are contributing to maintaining a group's positivity, with resulting momentum toward achieving future success.

Watching professionals who are on top of their game, such as athletes, pilots (like the famed Blue Angels), artists, musical performers, or record-breaking sales people, we find that they all spend considerable time reducing the importance of each failure, no matter how minor, to enhance their probability of success. They know full well that they just need to be better than their closest competitors to be successful. The margins become increasingly slimmer as the competition becomes increasingly more adept (as with Olympic runners and swimmers). To be adept, we mean squeezing out of each failure a nugget that can be used for building greater future success.

To enhance the probability of success, leaders also positively point to what others have accomplished in similar situations. In a recent *Harvard Business Review* article, Michael Tilson Thomas, the music director of the San Francisco Symphony, explained that his approach "is to be in tune with the people with whom I'm working. If I'm conducting an ensemble for the first time, I will relate what it is I want them to do to the great things they've already done."

Whatever strategy you choose, for you to be able to achieve sustainable positive growth and performance we recommend that you choose your cutoffs wisely. People will judge you largely on the base rate of authenticity you have built over time. You can also go to your authenticity in times where there is less confidence, hope, optimism, and resiliency.

As Michael Tilson Thomas pointed out, an orchestra leader's effectiveness and authenticity rests on "the orchestra's confidence in the conductor's insightful knowledge of the whole score and the orchestra's faith in the conductor's good heart, which seeks to inspire everyone to make music that is excellent, generous, and sincere." It is not just how many times you are right that will sustain growth and performance, although that is an important contributor. It's also how many times you went forth confident of success, even after you failed; how you remained positive again and again.

These positive effects on one's own and others' PsyCap has a long history of support in what has been called "transformational leadership." Transformational leaders convey a sense of confidence and hope that energizes their followers to perform what our colleague Bernie Bass labeled "performance beyond expectations."

What Bass suggests, and subsequently 20 years of research by Bruce and many others have now supported, is that the way transformational leaders behave encourages followers to reach into their reservoir of beliefs about what it is possible to accomplish. When transformational leaders do this, they come out believing more is always possible. They work with the assumption that there is a reserve of human potential that, once tapped into, will make the difference in achieving expected performance, or performance beyond expectations.

Tapping into the inevitable reserve human potential in your organization can contribute to achieving performance beyond expectations.

It's important to note that transformational leaders are by our definition authentic leaders. They maintain a belief that by continuously developing followers, they can contribute to sustainable growth and performance. In fact, these leaders were originally labeled transforming by James McGregor Burns, in his Pulitzer Prize–winning book *Leadership,* because they raised expectations sufficiently high enough to transform followers into leaders. We would argue that to do so, they had to build PsyCap in themselves and in turn in their followers.

Followers must have the belief that they can ascend to become leaders. We would also contend that ALD constitutes a similar transformation of individuals, through their PsyCap, into believing they are more capable of positively influencing others to achieve their full potential. However, using this PsyCap is not the central focus that one finds in transformational leaders.

BUILDING OUT PSYCAP IN FOLLOWERS

Your ALD process includes shaping and contributing to followers' PsyCap. If higher levels of PsyCap among your followers are known to result in higher levels of performance, then your ALD should include a plan for building it out. A significant part of this plan should include how you convey your own PsyCap to others, but that's only part of what enhances the PsyCap of followers.

Focusing on each follower who works directly for you now, could you judge their PsyCap level? How close were you in the exercise we asked you to do at the end of Chapter 7? How close do you think your estimate would be to theirs today? You may ask the same question about how close their judgment of your PsyCap is to your own.

Once you have in mind (substitute here self-awareness) the level of PsyCap in each follower, you might ask what you could do to enhance it. One of the simplest ways is to highlight what each of the followers has done well and figure out why. However, in building PsyCap this should not be simple feedback on success. As we have said in reviewing efficacy development research, we know it is not just a matter of being successful. In other words, attaining success does not equal efficacy. Rather, it's how people process the success that contributes to their subsequent confidence or efficacy.

As an example, telling followers they succeeded in the past because the conditions were right or they were lucky is not likely to positively impact on their future levels of self-efficacy. However, telling them how they specifically contributed to success through their talents and effort, along with positive recognition for doing so, can directly impact their level of not only confidence, but other PsyCap states such as optimism and hope.

To build resiliency, leaders will have to work with their followers on this efficacy building all the time. Leaders will have to positively reinforce learning from, and bouncing back and beyond, the moments that inevitably arise in life and at work that will be extremely challenging.

To build efficacy and resiliency, point out to followers exactly how they achieved past successes.

Go back and take a look at groups you have worked with what seemed to be doing quite well until a significant challenge arose. Often, groups with low PsyCap will fall apart when faced with such challenges. The result is destructive conflict, finger pointing, and performance meltdown.

We believe that building PsyCap in advance is a way of readying both the leader and the group of followers to sustain performance through difficult periods of sustained challenge. Indeed, this is the essence of our focus on moments that matter in relation to ALD. Leaders and followers who have developed their PsyCap to a high level from the inside out through life events or proactive ALD will have the basis for sustaining themselves through difficult times. At its core, this is what ALD is all about.

The plan in ALD is to work at building out PsyCap now. That way it can be expended when needed in the future and then replenished preparing for the next challenge and the one after that.

As part of ALD, you need to attend to building out PsyCap in order to sustain your own efforts and the efforts of those around you. How can this build-out be specifically accomplished? Here are some simple guidelines to follow:

- Reflect at the end or beginning of each week on what worked especially well for you and your people. What would you like to repeat to sustain this?
- Identify three positive drivers that contributed to what worked with your own and their performance.
- Provide yourself and relevant others with recognition and appreciation and take time to celebrate minor successes.
- Find out what form of recognition is most desired by every one of your followers. Do you know now? Most leaders make assumptions and don't really know. Therefore, the value of recognition is often not maximized when given.

- Consider how you allocate your time in terms of creating energy among your followers. When you're with them, make sure they have "their time" with you. Listen carefully to what they want to discuss with you. Giving them their time is a powerful way leaders can provide recognition. Effective recognition is as simple as "they know you know," rather than just plaques, banquets, and year-end bonuses.

- In terms of your own self-regulation, you need to know how you convey your confidence, hope, optimism, and resiliency to others. Each moment, day, week, month, and year, you exhibit behaviors that cue and serve as a model for followers to your PsyCap level. For example, fund managers often remark that the level of confidence and optimism exuded by the CEO directly affects their decision to invest. This same decision on whether to invest is taken by followers from you and the organization. As we discussed earlier, people are social learners, and therefore will learn by watching your leadership, often vicariously and based on what you model for them.

- Select what you can realistically and authentically develop through your confident, hopeful, optimistic, and resilient behavior. To be authentic or within the range of what would be considered authentic to you, you need to know where your own level of PsyCap is (that is, to be self-aware) in order to convey that PsyCap to others. There is a certain discipline to tracking your behavior, not unlike the example of Gallup's tracking of positivity, which we discussed at the beginning of the chapter.

- What Gallup's leadership believes is that if you "measure it," then "it" will be taken seriously. We would advocate the same position for yourself in terms of tracking PsyCap. For example, for one week track how many times, on average, you and your followers focus on positives versus negatives. Remember the study by positive psychologist Barbara Fredrickson at the University of Michigan, which showed that teams exhibiting about three positives to every negative were more effective at thinking through problems and issues rather than merely advocating one's position to the exclusion of others. What was your positive to negative ratio last week? Yesterday? What should it be tomorrow?

■ Ultimately, your own and your followers' PsyCap comes down to how positively you feel about yourself. You may not always be able to accomplish what is required, but how you deal with coming up short, or even failing, will determine how well-prepared you and your followers are for the next challenge. This starts with taking responsibility and owning the challenge, and getting others to do so as well. Through such responsibility and ownership, people build confidence in each other. It allows them to learn what each person contributed, where they fell short, and what they need to do to be successful.

PSYCAP AS A CORE FACTOR

In the last chapter and in this one, we have introduced you to psychological capital. All of the PsyCap states are commonly used in everyday language, have been discussed for many years, and have been studied extensively in clinical psychology and education. However, as pointed out in the introductory foundation for positive organizational behavior (POB) and PsyCap (psychological capital) in the last chapter, except for surface recognition, the application of confidence, hope, optimism, and resiliency is relatively unique to the workplace in general and organizational leadership in particular. Especially relevant and unique to ALD is that these individual positive states can be combined into a core factor of PsyCap.

In our study of the Chinese factory workers mentioned in the last chapter, we discovered something unique and revealing: Each of the criteria-meeting states of PsyCap was not as predictive of performance as they were in combination. In other words, the whole of PsyCap seems to contribute more than the sum of its parts. We are continuing to examine the combined PsyCap as a core factor in order to replicate and extend our findings.

Some interesting questions remain to be explored. For one, we need to determine whether a certain threshold or level has to be achieved for the individual states to contribute to the overall core factor of PsyCap. That is, can you remain hopeful and optimistic in the face of diminishing confidence? Will hope and optimism hold when one's confidence falls below a certain critical threshold level? Also, can you maintain a certain level of resiliency where levels of hope and optimism are eroded beyond a certain minimum level? How does hope compensate during the early stages of building optimism to take on a particular mission that you are not prepared to handle?

There are many such intriguing issues to consider that have not yet been fully researched or even observed in practice. We intend to do this in the coming years and will regularly update our findings at the Web site www.gli.unl.edu.

NEGATIVE PSYCAP

At this point we know enough about PsyCap to make the linkages to ALD. We know, for instance, that nothing can erode optimism, hope, and resiliency more than feelings of betrayal. Betrayal creates a near meltdown in PsyCap, a condition that is extremely difficult to recover with the same leadership and even with new leadership coming to the forefront. Once people have been betrayed by someone whom they trusted and with whom they identified, their energy is directed away from positive PsyCap to the negative cluster of mistrust, hopelessness, and, in the extreme, helplessness.

Organizations, like individuals, sometimes go through periods of abusive leadership, where trust is destroyed. It takes tremendous energy, and even courage, to move from negative to positive PsyCap. People quickly learn how to deceive and take advantage of a system that does not serve their needs.

Defense mechanisms are established that lead to avoidance in taking responsibility and ownership in one's organization, and this is by no means a natural state. It is in our view an illness caused by leaders and organizations. In the extreme, these conditions create what psychologists have called a "state of learned helplessness." This is where people learn that no matter what they do, nothing will work, so they eventually become immobilized, even when a positive opportunity arises. Such dysfunctional conditions go hand in hand with very negative PsyCap.

Positive PsyCap, on the other hand, involves leadership that has built trust, respect, transparency, and integrity into their organizational system. As opposed to being helpless, people have "learned helpfulness." Leaders and followers with high levels of PsyCap identify with the mission. The organizational mission and the leaders' core personal beliefs are interconnected. Remember the study of nurses we cited before: There was a strong, significant correlation between their overall PsyCap and the stated patient care mission of the hospital.

To fail means that *I* fail and *we* fail, and both options are equally unacceptable. We also wonder how the trust in nurses might factor into their level of PsyCap. In organizations where negative PsyCap predominates, someone else's failure is of no direct consequence to me and my performance—or is it? In fact, this failure may benefit my position.

Unfortunately, negative PsyCap may be the rule rather than the exception, at least in larger organizations. As we noted in Chapter

2, Gallup's polling of American workers over the last 30 years consistently indicates that confidence and trust in business has, on a scale from 0 to 100, hovered around 30 and below.

We believe the lack of trust and confidence in big business leadership translates into a greater likelihood of negative PsyCap. Additional supporting evidence from Gallup polls shows that nearly the same number of employees (about one-third) would be considered actively disengaged from their work. A large middle group of about 40 percent are neither engaged nor disengaged. These data suggest that the vast majority of the workforce is not actively engaged in their work, and engagement positively relates to positive PsyCap.

The number of actively disengaged employees is somewhat surprising, given the fact the U.S. workforce remains the most productive on earth. Thus, the good news this data indicates is that there is still tremendous residual productive performance that remains untapped.

According to the Gallup data, at least 40 percent of the American workforce could be more engaged and productive. What is also compelling about this data is that a large share of this engagement is directly attributable to the nature of leadership exhibited. Thus, we would argue that to more fully engage the workforce, we must engage managers in ALD. Engaged leaders and followers will result in more positive PsyCap, which in turn will, literally, "lead to" sustainable growth and performance.

MOVING FROM NEGATIVE TO POSITIVE PSYCAP

We have already suggested a number of guidelines in this chapter to enhance leader and follower PsyCap. To be more specific on how to get more engaged and move from negative to positive PsyCap, we still need to emphasize once again self- and collective awareness.

So we ask the question: What are the rules for engagement in your organization? We're not referring to the written rules, but rather, the informal, implicit ones that drive the organization.

Unlike successful sports teams (like those that win the NBA championship), we often have little idea of how best to engage each other. There is so much uncertainty and ambiguity surrounding engagement that the resulting mistrust, lack of transparency, and low levels of PsyCap are not unusual.

A concerted and focused effort is necessary to stay on top of engagement and PsyCap. Without careful monitoring and tracking—as is universally done with the financial capital indicators—PsyCap can get off target. Although we have recently conducted some questionnaire surveys in our research on PsyCap, we are confident in saying that no one has ever conducted a PsyCap audit in their company.

A discipline has not yet been created in our leaders to focus on the alternative and intangible PsyCap indicators. Clearly, researchers besides us have done related work where they focus on some positive organizational behaviors and how these contribute to performance. Nevertheless, applied to the real world, we are still very early in this game. However, there is sufficient research evidence underscoring the importance of intangibles, such as PsyCap, to sustaining growth and performance.

In a recent follow-up study of the companies listed in Collins's and Porras's best-selling book, *Built to Last,* the researchers reported that all of the 18 companies cited in the book were still in operation, and 10 of them were doing extremely well. However, the remaining eight were going through some tough transitions, most notably Disney's issues with board governance, CEO leadership under Michael Eisner, and declining business since the 9/11 attack. The study concluded that if you had invested in the stocks of the identified companies at the time the book was published, you would have received a whopping 900 percent return on your investment, even with the eight underperforming companies.

In a follow-up book by Jim Collins entitled *Good to Great*, he makes the point, building on his earlier work, that the great companies build and grow systematically over time, without leaps and bounds. Great companies work on the fundamentals and continue to grow a more positive outlook and culture, which results in learned helpfulness rather than learned helplessness.

Of course, simply building up PsyCap is not going to guarantee success, but not building it up over time certainly will guarantee a workforce that is under its full potential. Our research so far indicates that PsyCap will likely account for about 15 percent of the variance in performance. In a world of hypercompetition, this figure represents a significant advantage.

Starting at the individual level and moving on to what constitutes organizational culture, we should be able to provide reasonable estimates of PsyCap at individual, group, and organizational levels. Like tracking the Gallup daily indicator of positivity we spoke about earlier, it seems essential to make leadership aware of trends in PsyCap.

Monitoring the PsyCap can demonstrate how it contributes to predicting not only expected performance—especially to organizational leaders—but also the kind of performance that we have labeled "performance beyond expectations." It is in that range that transformational leaders—and now, we would argue, authentic transformational leaders—can contribute to sustainable growth and performance. This is where PsyCap can make a significant contribution to your ALD.

SOME TAKE-AWAYS FOR YOU TO CONSIDER

Our goal in this chapter was to go beyond traditional views of financial capital, and beyond even recently recognized human and social capital, and introduce what we call positive psychological capital, or simply PsyCap, into your ALD process. Why? Most organizations today can purchase the same technology, build and/or buy the same efficient processes and physical assets, and raise sufficient financial capital to engage customers in their markets. However, if they fail to positively engage their leaders' and associates' PsyCap, they have lost a sustainable competitive advantage.

In today's competitive battles, the most unique advantage that organizations have is their people; and specifically in our terms, their people's PsyCap. How organizations and their leaders invest in and leverage this capital may be the difference between success and also-rans.

Organizations should track their PsyCap in the same rigorous way they monitor their financial indicators.

Recently, Bruce was interviewing a group of managers who work for NASCAR's well-known Hendricks motors. One of the managers indicated that the key difference at the time of the race and prior to it is the psychological strengths (the PsyCap) of the team.

The Hendricks manager said the technology has become similar and available to all NASCAR competitors. Also, they were at the upper end of what this technology can squeeze out in terms of performance. Now, they were convinced that the psychology of the team would sustain its competitive performance over the course of a grueling eight-month schedule, where nearly every weekend is spent away from home. NASCAR has the longest schedule of any sport in the United States. Maintaining PsyCap would indeed seem critical to success. The way these managers described the importance of psychological strengths translates into what we called PsyCap and is part of the ALD process.

Here is a recap of some of the specific take-aways:

- PsyCap is made up of states, not fixed traits, and is therefore capable of being developed.

- PsyCap is a significant contributor to the ALD process.
- Your PsyCap will have both direct and indirect effects on the PsyCap of your followers, their followers, and ultimately on their clients, customers, and the success of the organization.
- You need to build-out and bank your PsyCap now for the challenges you will confront in the future.

FOR YOU TO DO ON YOUR ALD JOURNEY

We request that you now do two very specific activities.

First, we ask you to go to the Web site at www.e-leading.com, where you can take a short questionnaire that will produce a profile of each of your PsyCap states of confidence, hope, optimism, and resiliency. We also recommend that you have your followers log onto the same site, and then sit down when you both have had time to review your profiles to discuss the levels of PsyCap and how they can be further developed (as suggested in this chapter) and sustained over time. You might even want to fill out one form for your group as a whole to see how close you are to their average estimates.

Second, we would like you to take a look at your social network structure. This can be done either automatically by going to www.e-leading.com and using your PIN number found on the cover flap after our bios, where you and each of your followers will answer three questions. They are: Who gives you positive energy at work? Who challenges you? And: Whom do you go to for advice? You'll need to input all of the names you want everyone to choose from to answer these three questions. After you do this, what they will essentially see is a question followed by a list of all the names. The rater's job is to simply check the names that apply to that question. Once you and they have completed the three-item survey, three separate anonymous maps will be created that explain your social network structure in terms of positive energy, challenge, and advice.

It is important that you reassure each follower that no one will be identified in the map, even though you're using names in the survey. Indeed, the program randomly assigns a number to a name before the map is produced and sent to you. In that way, everyone may go to, say, number 9 in the map for advice, but no one will know who number 9 was, including you. Instructions on the site will take you through the overall process of creating this interesting and insightful social network map.

You can also create the network map mechanically by putting everyone's name on the board as the rows, and have the questions be the columns. Then you can go through as a group and put in the names that fit the description of each question. To do such an exercise requires tremendous trust, which is something that you will need to consider. We suggest that you at least go the confidential, automated route the first time.

Both the PsyCap profile and the network maps can effectively guide you on your ALD journey toward sustained performance, the focus of the next chapter.

LEADERSHIP NOTES

- *Like other resources in one's organization, the PsyCap of your workers can be developed over time.* A lot of attention is placed on growing the financial outcomes of an organization, but one of the main contributing factors to financial growth is the growth in social capital, and especially of PsyCap.

- By reviewing past successes to find out what worked and what didn't, a leader can build a sense of "learned helpfulness" versus learned helplessness. By spending time learning about what worked and what didn't, the leader is reinforcing the efficacy of his or her followers and the likelihood that they will take on more difficult challenges in the future.

■ *Take the time to track what is positive.* Often in organizations, the negative incidents outweigh the positives, and the negatives are more likely to be remembered. Compiling and recalling negative incidents can lead to the perceived ability of a group to be successful, and it can also deter them from taking on new challenges and adapting to change. Keeping the ratio of positives to negatives in check will help facilitate growth and development.

9

SUSTAINABLE AND
VERITABLE PERFORMANCE:
AN END GOAL OF ALD

AUTHENTIC LEADERSHIP naturally, and as portrayed so far, brings visions of trust, morality and ethics, psychological capital, and follower-building to its endgame. However, as we have stressed throughout—and it's a major differentiator from popular labels such as inspirational, servant, spiritual, or even ethical leadership—our meaning of authentic leadership also has performance as an end goal.

It's important, for authenticity, for us to qualify that performance for the ALD process must be both sustainable (lasting, over the long run) and veritable—that is, genuine, not the cook-the-books, look-good-at-all-costs style of performance that has emerged in recent years. In other words, we have strategically placed this chapter at the end of the book to remind you that the process of ALD is not the end in itself but that the aim of ALD is sustainable, veritable performance, as our formal definition in the beginning of the book indicated.

With this reminder of the importance of performance impact in ALD out of the way, let's start with some questions for you:

- What is your optimal performance? It may sound like a rather simple question to answer, but the more we thought about it, the more we realized that the answer is perhaps not so obvious.
- Is your performance based on just what you do at work? If so, what exactly do you do that is not impacted by someone else's performance?
- Do you consider your performance what you contribute to someone else's performance? If so, within what time interval?
- How do we measure your impact on others? Is your performance what you've done, what you're doing, or what you've done to accomplish something in the future?

As an example of the meaning and implications of the above questions, ask yourself: Is a teacher's performance measured by how much a student learns, how much a student applies, how much a student remembers, or how much a student teaches others? At what point does it seem appropriate to measure the impact of a teacher on a student's performance?

As with teaching, the same questions apply to leading. What measure of performance should we use to assess a leader's impact? Even more important, what should we consider optimal performance? Do we assess how leaders view what's possible and how they impact the possibilities envisioned in others?

In terms of ALD, do we assess what they have learned? Do we assess what they have changed in themselves or others? Do we assess how their unit performs? Do we assess how they contribute to the performance of other units? Or do we assess how their followers perform, influence others, and eventually learn to influence themselves over time?

Perhaps one of the quickest and least thought through decisions made by those involved in traditional leadership development relates to what, if at all, they typically choose to measure as the impact on performance. The common refrain over the years from colleagues of ours trying to show impact is: "What does the organization measure in terms of performance, and can we get access to those data?" If you are starting and ending at this point in terms of leadership development, we would argue that you will more than likely fail.

Unfortunately, what organizations typically measure does not usually help us to determine whether we have actually developed leadership—even in one leader! There clearly are a number of existing measures of performance that are important to a broad range of organizational constituencies. These include such metrics as all the well-established financial numbers, as well as market share, the number of new customers acquired, number of college graduates, total sales, return on investment, patents, wins versus losses, customer build-out, job creation, and so on. Yet very few of these directly connect to ALD. They do not connect because authentic leadership primarily creates the conditions for performance attainment, but does not necessarily directly impact the performance itself.

Consequently, as we discuss what constitutes performance, or especially optimal performance, we are more keenly interested in the metrics that connect more directly to the impact of ALD. These in turn impact positively on the other more traditional performance metrics. Why? Because you simply cannot have ALD without knowing your performance impact points to be targeted in the future. Even though we are discussing this toward the end of the book, it should be emphasized that performance impact points need to be the very first step in the ALD process, not the last.

Effective leadership creates the "conditions for success."

THE NATURE AND LEVEL OF PERFORMANCE IMPACT

We have been exploring what you can do as part of the ALD process to enhance your effectiveness. Now we want to identify some specific impact points of performance we want you to target, depending on where you are in the ALD process. At a minimum, these impact points can be thought of as milestones to track ALD. They also can be part of the ALD process itself, in the sense that they can be catalysts for ALD.

How we define performance impact for ALD can be simply depicted as comprising the two-by-five matrix shown in the chart below. Notice that we depict both the nature of performance (typical and extraordinary) and what we will call its "level of impact" (at intra- and inter-individual, group/team, organizational, and community levels):

NATURE AND LEVEL OF PERFORMANCE IMPACT

NATURE	LEVEL				
	Intra-individual	Inter-individual	Group/Team	Organization	Community
Typical Range					
Extraordinary Range					

Let's start with the nature of performance, or the rows. Most performance measures in organizations tap into the "typical range" of what is expected of employees. This can range dramatically depending on the nature of the organization and the leadership challenges it has had or is currently confronting.

What is typical performance for the most elite special forces unit in the U.S. Army, for example, is not necessarily within the typical range of infantry platoons. What is typical performance for a trauma team in a prestigious hospital system is not typical for the neighborhood clinic or small-town hospital medical team. The typical output of a project team at H-P or Microsoft may not be the same as the typical output of a project team of an electronics assembly factory.

Deciding what is typical and what is extraordinary for your work is an exercise we suggest you do with yourself and with those who contribute to your performance impact points. When was the last time you told a story about extraordinary performance at work? And we don't mean extraordinarily bad! You should make an agreed upon distinction between the typical and these extraordinary performances so they can be used as impact points in your own and others ALD.

Making matters more difficult, however, it's important to keep in mind that the threshold for typical also changes over time. These changes depend on your competitors' aspirations and performance achievements, as well as your own aspirations. For instance, as a story on Amazon's Jeff Bezos noted, "It's one thing to be a data junkie who just looks at history. Jeff takes risks, and he changes and changes."

Simple examples include the typical performance maintenance schedule for most new cars, which now requires that you change the spark plugs every 100,000 miles, when 30 years ago spark plugs were changed every several thousand miles. Similarly, the turn-around time for ordering new products has been slashed from what were months a few years back to days or hours now, depending on the industry. People undergoing open heart surgery 15 years ago spent weeks in the hospital recovering. Today they spend days, and are up on their feet the next day.

Leading edge firms set the standard for extraordinary performance. Dell Computer will turn over its inventory more than 100 times per year, while their competitors do so less than 30 times per year. We suspect in a few years 100 will become typical for this industry and something like 300 might be extraordinary performance. Indeed, throughout this book we have argued that ALD is becoming increasingly important because what is considered extraordinary performance in an industry has become typical in a shorter time than previously. This moving target puts increasing pressure on organizational leaders to develop adaptive and resilient workforces.

Extraordinary shifts in performance expectations in almost every sector of the economy have caused organizations to accelerate nearly every aspect of their business processes. This is true from order acquisition to supply chain management to delivery. To achieve these outlandish expectations requires organizational leaders to maintain consistently high levels of PsyCap (confidence, hope, optimism, and especially resiliency). As we said in the last two chapters, this PsyCap is part of your ALD.

How have you articulated the standards for extraordinary performance?

PERFORMANCE IMPACT POINTS FOR ALD

To reiterate, if you are only talking about leadership development in the abstract and not connecting it to specific performance impact points, then we feel you are missing a very important opportunity. Furthermore, without such specific performance points, you will not be able to sustain investments in your own and others ALD.

As an example, unless you can demonstrate performance impact, you may not survive budget cuts. In other words, surviving downsizing or cuts in training and development costs could be used for estimating ALD's minimal, but not maximum, worth.

As we indicated above, your performance impact points for ALD range from typical to extraordinary. We would now challenge you to consider that everyone in your organization should know two things about performance.

What constitutes the range of typical performance? What would constitute extraordinary performance? Do you presently know what constitutes each? Do you know if others around you know? And, how are you progressing within your current range of typical performance to reach extraordinary performance?

Here are a few specific examples of shifts in performance expectations from what used to be extraordinary and has now become typical.

- Overnight shipping has changed the standard time we expect to receive decision outcomes, products, test results, contracts, etc.
- Pictures are taken now and sent to relatives before they have even returned home, creating a paradigm shift in the film processing and printing industry.
- MBA degree programs have gone from a two-year format to, in some instances, nine months.
- Developing a new car concept from idea to production has gone down from five years to less than two.
- We can get acknowledgment of our bills being paid within the same hour.
- Flight arrangements can be changed in minutes online.
- We can order new clothes, have them custom fit, and shipped to our homes in days or less.
- Financial investors expect returns in weeks, down from years in the past.
- New advanced computer technology can create an entire movie set without ever leaving the production facility, transforming the way movies are made.
- Software developers work online 24 hours a day in three to four locations around the world, drastically reducing times to develop and deploy new software.

What should have motivated organizational leaders to consider how they process what needs to be done to achieve these new typical performance standards? Indeed, in every area it can be determined what is currently typical, what is within the extraordinary range, and the half-life of this extraordinary performance until it becomes typical.

The pressure to perform across all sectors of the economy has raised the bar on leadership to such a high level that there is now a tremendous challenge facing organizations to develop leaders faster and better. For ALD, we have entered into a phase of required lean development. This is similar to the lean manufacturing processes that have pulled out most of the unnecessary costs in our manufacturing systems.

To the degree that the performance standards have shifted (i.e., extraordinary has become typical), naturally, the requirements for leaders and followers must also shift. If products and services are needed faster, and at the same time of higher quality, then the organizational systems that produce them must also advance in terms of development. Has yours?

How have your leadership development interventions changed to accommodate these accelerated performance expectations? Does your organization start its focus on leadership development emphasizing performance impact points? We want you to focus on these performance questions because, we argue, what drives the people who drive the organization and its performance is ALD. Therefore, you must know what constitutes typical performance today and five years from now. At the same time, you need to consider the shifting standards for extraordinary performance.

It should be clear now that performance is indeed a moving target. Yet, at any one point in time, we can and should differentiate typical performance from extraordinary performance. In doing so, we are then able to link what we are developing to what we expect to impact. We need to determine what people should typically accomplish versus what would be considered extraordinary accomplishment.

As an example, even after 25 years of concerted efforts through the TQM movement to lead organizations to produce higher quality products and services, extraordinary quality is considered Six Sigma. This means six standard deviations out statistically. Today, very few organizations operate at the Six Sigma level. However, most organizational leaders would agree that typical quality standards must now be at least two to three sigma or standard deviations up from the average to become competitive and even survive.

LEVELS OF PERFORMANCE IMPACT

Looking back at the columns in our performance matrix shown earlier, when you think about the impact of ALD, you should consider the level at which you expect to show positive performance results. So, when doing the exercise on what constitutes typical and extraordinary performance, we now need you to also consider the level of impact as follows:

- *Intra-individual impact.* At this level, we expect to have an impact on the individual leader to perform better at something. For example, the leader may focus on the ratio of how many positive to negative comments she makes each day. By doing this, she is determining the level of positivity in the unit. Her ALD has a performance impact if the number of positives to negatives shifts from, say, one-to-one to three-to-one. This change may constitute typical performance. However, going to six-to-one may be an optimal level (rather than all positives) and end up in the extraordinary range of performance compared to the typical ratio distributed by most other leaders.

  The increased self-awareness in ALD about levels of PsyCap (e.g., confidence, hope, or optimism) can be considered an intra-individual performance metric. The specific impact points at this intra-individual level are in leaders' working self-concept or model. Leaders may have these performance points in their head about the importance of creating a positive climate and in their behavior and actions (i.e., the positive/negative ratio and/or the level of PsyCap).

■ *Inter-individual impact.* At the inter-individual level, in the ALD process the importance of examining what constitutes the most important form of recognition for each follower has been emphasized. For example, we might expect the individual leader to develop a clearer understanding of what each follower desires in terms of recognition within one month of working with followers. The leader can make sure to get followers what they most desire (such as recognition) when they perform well. Inter-individual impact may be providing such recognition in line with each follower's expectation exactly when it can have the most motivating effect on performance. This inter-individual level of impact could push performance from the typical into the extraordinary range.

■ *Group-level impact.* How a group coordinates and accomplishes its work may be a performance impact point for ALD. Specifically, this performance point could be used by a leader who is working on encouraging her group to align their goals to both their own and the organization's goals. In this case, coordination time would be a useful metric for the performance impact of the work group. Another example would be to examine the social network structure of a group over time. This would include examining the leader's efforts to motivate and reinforce members of the group to trust one another enough to share valuable knowledge and information that can accelerate performance processes.

Group impact may also be reflected in the transparency the leaders create through their behavior and actions. This may result in followers willing to offer their best, creative ideas, even when they challenge the basic assumptions of the leader. Then, how long it takes for a group to generate the next big idea and to implement the process that produces the products or services could be an impact point to monitor for the overall group. Extraordinary levels of performance may be reflected and measured in the fastest turnaround times from idea to product/service to process transformation.

■ *Organizational-level impact.* Usually, when we are at the organizational level, we need to focus on strategic level leadership. For example, we might examine the level of service excellence at every facility within the organization. This, in turn, is tied to the strategic leader's goal of every single customer's moment that matters. To implement the improvement in customer service, the CEO may begin a campaign to have employees leave every customer engagement with some evidence that the customer was extraordinarily satisfied (which might be seen in direct or indirect objective feedback).

Examples of "out of the box" metrics of organizational performance impact would be Jeff Bezos commenting: "Sometimes we measure things and see that in the short term they actually hurt sales, and we do it anyway." He has enough PsyCap built up in his ALD process to say, "You have to use your judgment. We know this is a feature that's good for customers. Let's do it." Alternatively, another senior leader may measure performance impact by how long it takes one team to take another team's contract proposal and adapt it to a customer's needs. We can also assess the performance impact based on every employee who has some direct or indirect connection to the customer. This employee often has about the last opportunity to provide a positive moment with a particular customer, at any point in time. This employee-customer moment becomes an impact point for organizational level performance.

- *Community-level impact.* Consider a city that has a number of top community leaders who have over the last 20 years raised the city's standard of living, quality of life, and attractiveness. They may be recognized as one of the top 10 in the country. The goal these leaders then set is to develop the next generation of community leaders to sustain the current momentum well beyond the time they themselves are still active in leadership roles. Thus, they develop a two-year intervention to attract and develop an entirely new generation of leaders. Those identified may be nearly ready to assume leadership roles in the community, and the ALD process is designed to bring them to the forefront faster. In 10 years the present leaders want to look back and see top level leaders on all civic initiatives. They want to see the economic growth indices of the city advancing on an even higher performance curve than when they turned it over. In less than two years these former leaders will have designed and successfully executed a citywide succession planning process that had community-level performance impact.

One of the important points we want to convey with these examples of the various levels of performance impact is a basic principle that we feel underlies leadership in general and ALD in particular. In summary, to develop leadership, you have to start with the performance impact point you desire. This impact, however, has two dimensions: the nature of the performance (typical or extraordinary) and the level (intra- and inter-individual, group, organizational, and community). You need to know where you're going to end up on both dimensions so you can more accurately configure to accelerate the development of leadership.

To optimally develop leadership, start with the performance impact point you want to hit in the future.

Too often, leadership development is first and foremost about the individual leader (intra-individual level). Then, as an afterthought, it is about followers, groups, units, organizations, and communities. This may be fine, if that is indeed the desired impact point. However, in most instances simply developing the individual leader by just focusing on intra-individual performance change is not sufficient.

We find it curious that very few traditional leadership development interventions have examined what might be considered the ultimate impact point of its desired leadership development. Most often this is a change in followers—any change whatsoever. It seems perplexing to us that most leadership development interventions track changes in the leader when we expect the most important changes to be evident in followers. How about the leadership development programs you've participated in? Can you specify what, if anything, has been tracked?

To focus on follower impact we need to blend across levels the performance impact points we expect to obtain from our developmental interventions. For example, leaders who get their positive to negative ratio of comments up to 3/1 could expect to observe followers more willing to engage each other in idea generation, exploring alternative perspectives, and coming to creative solutions. In this example, changing the performance of the leader from an intra-individual perspective is ultimately demonstrated in the way followers think and interact with each other. So why not measure changes in followers when we try to develop the leader? And, more to the point, what is the causal link between the change in the leader and the follower whose performance level we expect to change?

These links between leader development and change in followers are the basis for sustainable and veritable performance at individual, group, organizational, and community levels. Yet, the higher up we go in terms of levels of impact, the more complicated these links become to identify and understand, though they are not at all impossible to attain. What we mean is that at the very highest levels of organizations—and don't let anyone suggest that we have eliminated hierarchies completely—the way leaders impact many of their followers is indirect and through various organizational processes.

THE INDIRECT IMPACT OF ALD: CORE ORGANIZING PRINCIPLES AND VALUES

As we have said, every great organization has a core organizing principle and value that in the broadest sense guides almost everything the organization accomplishes. For a company like 3M, for instance, it has been innovation. For an organization like NASA it has been exploration. For the Gallup Organization, it has been focusing on people's strengths. And for a fast growing restaurant chain called Mimi's Café, it is POS, or "positively outrageous service."

Leaders can use these core principles as a way to sustain or change their organizations. For example, when the now departed Carly Fiorina first took over HP and the famous "HP Way," she knew things needed to change. As knowledgeable observer Marjorie Scardino noted: "Fiorina adapted the HP way to her way. Taking 'Invent!' as the rallying cry, she invented a new future." She led HP on many fronts to attain organizational level performance impact points in terms of modernizing how HP did business, how it was organized, and how it viewed the outside world and unmet opportunities (e.g., powering the core of the digital household). Unfortunately, since her ouster at HP, Fiorina has also become an example of how difficult it is to accomplish change.

After challenging leaders to think of a core organizing principle, we suggest they then need to focus on the core organizing value that typifies the principle underlying their business. In our experience, most organizational leaders seem compelled to have a whole list of values. One just doesn't seem sufficient. We disagree.

We suggest you start with your core organizing value, such as innovation, safety, exploration, caring, strengths, outrageous service, and/or transparency. Now think about how you would drill this value down throughout your organization so it becomes each individual's primary value and part of their working self-concept.

John Browne, CEO of British Petroleum, for example, pushes the value of BP being environmentally conscious and "green in everything we do and say." To back up this core principle, he was the first leader in the oil industry to acknowledge the problem of climate change, but also used this environmental concern as a performance impact point. He claims BP's efforts at controlling emissions have added $650 million of market value to the company in three years, for an investment of just $20 million. Do you see what we mean by the indirect impact that performance leadership can have?

The indirect impact can also be demonstrated by the founders of organizations. A founding leader of an organization usually brings a particular "pet" value to the formation of that organization. Indeed, the organization over time becomes a hologram, so to speak, of the leader and his or her core value. The leader establishes the organization on some founding principles.

An example of the impact of a founding value would be David Neeleman, mentioned earlier, starting JetBlue Airways in 2000 with his stated value of "bringing humanity back to flying." Such a founding or organizing principle becomes part of all the exchanges in the organization—the way things are done. So far the success of JetBlue is living proof of this leader's founding value.

Based on the core organizing principle or value, the leader establishes the nature of performance that is desired. Over time, the organization may grow to perhaps thousands of employees stretched around the globe. Now, let's assume, even with this growth, the organization stays true to the core value and principle. How? The leadership of the organization made it their responsibility to be the stewards of the value, to retell the stories that exemplified it, and to reinforce it through their performance evaluation systems.

Let's use JetBlue again as an example. In its obsession for customer service, there is the well-known story concerning the time when most airlines shut down in the blackout of August 2003. The whole company knows Neeleman drove out to the tarmac to beg for fuel to keep his planes in the air to serve customers. This type of leadership is credited for making JetBlue the first low-cost airline since deregulation to so quickly become a major carrier. It now has more than $1 billion in revenues.

Every great organization has a core organizing principle that guides every great thing it does and accomplishes.
Perpetuating the founding value over time and growth represents an indirect impact of leadership. Nevertheless, as shown by the Neeleman example, it is perhaps one of the most important roles that leaders perform.

ALD can drive into every employee's definition of himself or herself what their organization most values. In our experience, almost all organizations state their values somewhere. However, rarely do they drill them down to such an extent that every employee knows exactly how those values guide their big decisions or their day-to-day job behavior.

We're both familiar with many organizations that "get religion" around developing a set of values. They typically expend a lot of energy writing and rewriting the values. However, they spend little time reinforcing these values so they can be seen in the way leaders and associates throughout the organization think, behave, and evaluate. Why? They usually generate way too many values to focus on and reinforce.

Unlike other areas of business, most organizations' values are not prioritized. One example we came across recently was Citigroup. A year or so ago this firm had no less than 26 values listed, but now has subsequently collapsed them into seven or eight. We maintain that you cannot recall, nor successfully reinforce, seven or eight values with a level of consistency that is warranted for building high performing systems, let alone 26!

Typically, we have found that the espoused values of organizations are just abstract ideals ("Fly the friendly skies of United") without sufficient ties to what the leaders consider typical and extraordinary performance. The values are positioned as feel-good ideals, but they're only reinforced if people can see how they are displayed in the decisions, actions, and behaviors of their leaders (in the case of United, leaders with pay increases who ask for pay cutbacks from operating personnel, versus Jet Blue's Neeleman driving out on the tarmac to beg for fuel).

Values will never stick and have the intended performance impact if they are not recognized and rewarded in tangible ways. In fact, we've found that if you want to give leaders an exercise to create a high level of cynicism among their followers, simply have them generate a set of "core" values the leaders have no plan to reinforce.

By the way, generating and publicizing the values, whether you have a plan to reinforce them or not, will still result in people in your organization judging how consistent you are against those values. So once they go up on the wall, they will begin judging. Are you ready?

Just think about this for a moment. Type in www.enron.com and you will find integrity as one of their espoused core values. It was their core value before their meltdown, and it is their core value after the meltdown. Frankly, it's hard for us to take such a value seriously given Enron's history and the thousands of employees and businesses who were screwed by the leaders of that organization.

A contrasting example to Enron might be Daniel Vassella, CEO of the Swiss-based Novartis, in the embattled drug industry. Although he admits that his first responsibility is to his investors, he also led the firm to be one of the first to commit to the U.N.'s Global Compact, which requires the highest environmental, human rights and labor standards wherever they operate. His approach led well-known Harvard professor and business book author Rosabeth Kanter to note that "he epitomizes a kind of leadership that puts equal emphasis on the social value created by the product and its economic value."

Another example is the Body Shop founder Anita Roddick, who established this successful firm and referred to its purpose as follows: "To dedicate our business to the pursuit of social and environmental change." As part of their mission and values, the firm has focused on using all natural ingredients in its products.

The Body Shop has also taken a stand against using animal testing for experimentation with new cosmetics. Roddick's leadership of the organization has been wrapped around this cause, and in many ways it has distinguished it in a crowded and highly competitive industry. Thus, in terms of defining their performance impact point, like the Novartis example, the Body Shop includes a social agenda. This clearly differentiates it from other companies in that industry. This social agenda requires that the leaders chosen and developed value—that "reason for being"—is demonstrated in their behavior and actions every day and in every moment of interaction.

There is another side to the Body Shop story. A few years back, several critical reports were released in England that indicated that the Body Shop was not living up to its well-known core ideal or organizing principle. Several investigations had concluded that in fact they were using products that were developed based on animal testing. In addition, their employment practices in overseas facilities were judged abysmal. Whether these charges are true or not, they do point out that the trouble with defining oneself so specifically around a core organizing value is that you have to live up to it. If you don't, you will unravel very quickly. This, of course, happened with the then recognized top accounting firm in the world, Arthur Andersen. They went out of business very quickly because of their highly questionable, if not illegal, audits with Enron.

When we are asked to trust any organization or leader based on their founding core principles, and then they violate our trust, the unraveling is lightning quick. It takes very hard work and a long time to build an impeccable reputation, but it can be destroyed very fast.

Remember our example in an early chapter of a letter Warren Buffett sent to the CEOs of Berkshire Hathaway's companies? In it he indicated that it took Berkshire some 37 years to establish its image of high ethical business practices, and that in 37 seconds it could all be lost if any of the executives chose to make a decision that they knew was questionable, if not unethical.

Living up to one's core organizing value establishes an impact point that will significantly determine the nature of one's business growth and sustainability. Michael Dell's founding core values on selling direct to consumers at low prices instead of innovating has moved his firm from PCs to desktops and notebooks, then to servers and storage, and now to printers and flat-screen TVs. Living up to this core organizing value has had a performance impact of over $40 billion in sales (which he wants to realistically double in a few years).

We would propose that ALD is the process that leaders need to go through (as an example, Dell's number two, Kevin Rollins, who is scheduled to take over) in order to understand the centrality of the core value. The ALD process incorporates how the core value is manifested in every leader and follower's actions and behaviors.

The range of cynicism we often see around the establishment and execution of core values reflects the fact that no one believes they are anything more than hollow, paper values. Worse yet, these paper values are frequently contradicted and cannot even be recalled by most people in the organization. Indeed, in one very large Fortune 500 company we are familiar with, the employees could not even agree within their geographical region, let alone across regions, what the most important core value was. At the other extreme, some organizational leaders know full well the core value and then blow it, as seen in the decisions they too often make, contradicting what the value represents.

As in manufacturing processes, consistency is the key to quality core values. Specifically, we are talking about the consistency in the quality of relationships that are based on trust, and the alignment of behavior with the core value.

Contrasting corporate values with national values, most would agree that the core organizing value for the United States over the years is liberty. This value is a reflection of the country's high level of individuality, and it has been reinforced, debated, and litigated almost every day since the beginning. We can see it in the behavior of entrepreneurs, just as we can see it in the behavior of a lawyer defending his client's individual rights, or in a small town's or big city's right to determine its own destiny against the will of the federal government.

Liberty is our organizing value. Even though it is sometimes violated, it is something that becomes automatic in our thinking. It is also in the thinking of people who immigrate here and over time become more individualistic, like the rest of us. So we would suggest that the ALD program for the value of liberty occurs in our schools, legislatures, the press, courts, and in our organizations and homes.

It is very rare to find in today's organizations a core value so well understood as liberty. The lack of understanding of its own core value in many organizations hurts its ability to rapidly advance from typical to extraordinary performance. Why? Because the core value defines who you are as an organization, community, and/or nation.

Like in individual leadership development, if an organization does not have sufficient self-awareness of who it is, how could it possibly regulate the directions it wants to pursue? And if it can't self-regulate, it cannot have focus. And if an organization doesn't have focus, there is no way it's going to achieve extraordinary performance. The exceptions would be that of JetBlue and Dell Computer, which we used as examples of firms that know their core value and have attained extraordinary performance.

ALD AND VERITABLE PERFORMANCE

We have taken the position throughout our discussion of ALD that life is the most authentic leadership development program. What we develop and call leadership interventions are meant to positively accelerate life's program. Now we have added to our discussion of ALD the end goal of performance and the qualifiers of sustained and veritable, or genuine, true performance.

Increasingly, we hear leaders in many organizations lament about what constitutes such true performance. Part of this discussion stems from the recently widely publicized corporate ethical meltdowns and questionable and/or illegal audits. They did not tell us anything close to the veritable or true value of the organizations involved. Yet at the same time, this is because of the changing nature of economies and competitive pressures around the globe. It has become increasingly more complex to describe what constitutes veritable performance at any level of impact. The challenge for ALD is to identify as closely as one can the veritable performance impact point you are attempting to achieve in order to enable leaders to track real progress over time.

Let's return to the question we asked you to consider at the beginning of the chapter regarding what constitutes typical and extraordinary performance in your work. What would be the most genuine measures of typical and extraordinary performance for you? Now, how would you develop someone to take on those typical and extraordinary performance challenges? Essentially, that is a key link we have been looking for throughout this book. And at this point, we want to make sure it is fully and deeply understood by you, so you can go off and apply it on your own. To do so, we will tell you a story.

We want you to think about someone you have read about or met. This should be someone who has achieved something extraordinary. However, they did not achieve this on their own, but achieved something extraordinary through someone else. What we typically witness is the end point of a whole lot of moving parts that resulted in such an achievement. Yet, if you closely examine what transpired, you will usually learn about the extraordinary process that preceded the extraordinary accomplishment.

THE STORY OF WARREN BUFFETT AS AN AUTHENTIC LEADER

For us, one such extraordinary story involves how Warren Buffett built Berkshire Hathaway over the years into the most successful investment vehicle in history. He is now setting out to do the same with his foundation. We conveyed in earlier chapters some of the moments in his life that he relayed to us firsthand, moments that shaped his thinking about his leadership and how he worked with others to achieve his dreams. Buffett started with the following points:

- He has never bought an organization from people who did not love their business. In fact, almost all of the CEOs who came with the organizations he has acquired are still in the role of CEO, and still loving their business.

- He wanted to live up to the type of interactions he observed in his father's work with customers in his grocery store, where he never saw his father treat anyone without the utmost respect, dignity, and honesty.
- He views himself as much an artist as a financial investor, and the building of Berkshire as his canvas to paint on.
- He has people around him he loves to work with, and he trusts them without question. The turnover in his office is zero.
- He places trust in the leaders of companies he buys, and said there have been some companies he has never even visited. Berkshire has a full-time staff, including Warren himself, of approximately 18 employees, who are running this huge conglomerate of businesses and 130,000 employees.
- His contracts to buy complex businesses are rarely more than a couple of pages, and in many instances the negotiation to buy the business lasted little more than an hour's time in his office.
- He demands honesty, transparency, and high ethics in all of his business dealings, and relishes simplicity in how a business should operate. For example, Jeff Bezos relates one of his favorite Warren Buffettisms, as he calls them: "You can hold a rock concert and that can be successful, and you can hold a ballet and that can be successful, but don't hold a rock concert and advertise it as a ballet. If you're very clear to the outside world that you're taking a long-term approach, then people can self-select in."
- He leads by example, offers advice as requested, and provides the bare minimum guidance by mainly focusing on the importance of doing business honestly and making money . . . in that order. Wall Street observer James Cramer recently noted

that Buffett should be Exhibit A in all the white collar prosecutions under way: "Ladies and gentlemen of the jury, despite the protestations of the defendant that he didn't know that what he did was wrong, we present you with Warren Buffett, who made fortunes without cutting a single corner, without being greedy, and without a whiff of scandal."

- He has a sense of humor about life that makes him totally genuine. In responding to a question posed by a student in our class, "What happens when you are dead?" Buffett replied that he hoped that when the minister was speaking at his funeral, he would start the sermon out by saying, "Warren Buffett . . . he was very, very, very old when he died!"

- He has said that one of his major goals in life is to make as much money as he can in order to endow the foundation he and his late wife set up to take on the "big bat" issues in the world such as nuclear proliferation. He said that if his foundation had been around in the late 1950s and early 1960s, he hoped it would have financially supported the Civil Rights movement, which in his view had no "investment bankers" to support it.

- When he came to the University of Nebraska he was speaking to our students, who now occupy the chairs that he sat in as an undergraduate in our college. He indicated he would not leave until the last question had been asked and answered, and he did just that, and then went to lunch at Dairy Queen, one of his companies.

Warren Buffett has created enormous wealth for many, many stockholders and nearly everyone in his extended family. Many of these individuals have taken that wealth and donated it to worthy causes. It almost seems like good money has been invested in good causes, if one were to look at his record through an idealistic lens.

Buffett's philanthropic orientation is reflected in what he most admires about his longtime friend Bill Gates. He recently stated, "Bill Gates is one of a kind. No, I'm not talking about the Bill who in a short period developed one of the most innovative and successful businesses in history. I'm talking about the Bill who, along with his wife Melinda, has in a far shorter length of time developed and funded the most innovative and successful foundation in history."

In his best-selling book on *Authentic Leadership,* Bill George is on record as stating that great historical leaders such as George Washington, Abraham Lincoln, Winston Churchill, Franklin Roosevelt, Margaret Thatcher, Martin Luther King, Mother Theresa, John F. Kennedy, and a few business leaders such as David Packard, all had very different styles, but all were, in his meaning, authentic. In contrast, although we use various leaders to demonstrate points we are making, we have been hesitant throughout this book to cite this or that leader as being an authentic leader.

We have been reluctant to identify specific authentic leaders for two reasons. First, we are truly interested in authentic leadership *development* as opposed to authentic leaders per se. We have wanted to stay on task with our focus on the developmental process. Second, to label someone as authentic who is still alive is risky. Historians often wait decades to thoroughly evaluate a President's accomplishments, since over time the truth generally comes out. There are too many smart people around for the truth not to eventually emerge.

At this point, however, perhaps it is time for us to go on record as believing that Warren Buffett does indeed represent what we define as an authentic leader. Important for the purpose of this book, we also believe his authentic leadership was developed in line with what we have been describing as life's ALD process. We say so with some confidence since he was born in, grew up in, graduated from of our college here at the University of Nebraska, and stayed in the heart of the heartland, and, therefore, he must be authentic . . . right?

Kidding aside, most important in our touting of Buffett as an authentic leader is because he has, for the last 50 years or so, clearly demonstrated all of the qualities we would hope to see in such leaders described as authentic. As Wall Street commentator James Cramer recently noted:

> He's our Shakespeare, a financial writer who puts everyone else to shame. He's our Joe DiMaggio, with a stock-market hit streak that will never be bettered. He's also our George Bailey, the too-good-to-be-true capitalist. And, if he weren't such a nice guy, we would all be jealous of him instead of in awe of him and his plainspoken nature.

Buffett has proven to be totally genuine, aware of himself in every sense, and grounded in a strong core value of high ethics. He is transparent in his dealings with others, positive, optimistic, hopeful, trustworthy, and honest. He has chosen to pass up great business opportunities that did not meet his core organizing principle (witness his passing on the ride up of the tech stocks because he did not understand them, but also not being on the crashing ride down of those who thought they did). So, he has demonstrated his convictions in situations where he could have profited enormously, but chose to stay on what we have been referring to as the thin white bright line.

BUFFETT AS AN EXAMPLE OF ALD

In terms of ALD, we can see that Warren learned the value of building enduring relationships as being at the core of his business model. Obviously, he knows how to value a company from a financial perspective. However, he also says you can tell a lot about people and their nature by the balance sheets they report.

Many leaders and consulting firms want to be the "trusted advisor" for this or that industry. Warren Buffett never set out to be the trusted advisor for anyone, and yet not a week seems to go by that one or another CEO doesn't come to Omaha to meet the "Oracle."

Warren Buffett seems to have learned from observing those he has respected and, as he has indicated, reading about others. He learned how fragile relationships are that are based on trust, yet how resilient such relationships can be as well. On the fragile side, he found you simply cannot violate the public trust. On the resilient side, there is nothing more resilient than the deep trust one has for another, which no legal contract can achieve. This is why Buffett's contract negotiations are so short—they are based largely on developing trusted relationships.

Authentic leaders achieve the status of "trusted advisors" in their organizations.

Warren likes to talk about the importance of people in his life who helped shape his philosophy. These important others include early teachers, professors in undergraduate and graduate school, his father, and business colleagues he has grown to respect, like Bill Gates, one of his best friends. Indeed, not a year after his wife passed away, Warren replaced her on his board of directors of Berkshire Hathaway with Gates. This one act on Buffett's part has caused us (and we are sure many others) to think deeply about the public and private depictions of Bill Gates.

In essence, that Buffett chose Gates to replace his deceased wife on the board of Berkshire Hathaway in and of itself might be enough for us to question what some have said about Bill Gates's character. In a nutshell, that's the power of Buffett's authenticity in terms of evaluating the qualities of other people whom he deems of character and integrity. Interesting how this example of choosing Gates parallels what we all value in how he judges the quality of organizations to invest in over time.

Warren appears to have a level of self-awareness that has allowed him to grow over his life to reach his possible selves. When meeting him now in his early 70s, he appears youthful in his energy, thought, and imagination. He clearly seems to enjoy his life, or as he said, he loves it.

As we related in an early chapter, he also provided that high bar standard for what constitutes authentic leadership from a "moment" he had with Rose Blumkin, the small, Jewish woman who came to Omaha, Nebraska, from the Holocaust. She built one of the most successful furniture businesses in the United States before she passed on at 101 years of age while still active in the company. If you remember, we told you she informed Warren that success is "how many people would choose to hide you" if your life and their life depended on it. As we said, Warren jokingly told our students that most rich people he has met over the years had kids who would be the first to reveal their location. But he quickly added that was not true of his children, and from all accounts we know that his statements are veritable.

As we look to Warren Buffett's extraordinary career accomplishments, in many ways we are seeing only the very earliest stages of performance impact from his ALD process. Yes, he is currently the second richest man in the world, next to Bill Gates. However, he has indicated that when he is done "borrowing all of that money from the economy," he will turn it over to the Buffett Foundation.

Again, like the foundation his friend Gates established, the Buffett Foundation will instantly become one of the largest philanthropic foundations in the world. The foundation based on his wishes will go after what we said earlier he calls the "big bat" issues of the time, whatever they may be. And, like his relationships with his CEOs, he has indicated that the founding board he has chosen to serve on the foundation will have much greater wisdom than he can provide from six feet under the ground. In other words, he intends to leave it up to them, with only minimal guidelines, to establish the agenda for supporting the "big bat" issues.

As we try to examine Warren Buffett's ALD process, we obviously know of or can only speculate about a small number of moments that have shaped this authentic leader. Yet one of the clear consistencies across these moments that mattered was that they were largely positive, not life's tragic events. We chose Buffett as our example because of his authenticity and also because he seems to have been able to take advantage of many of life's positive moments in his ALD.

SOME TAKE-AWAYS FROM THIS CHAPTER

In sum, we have argued that without specifying what constitutes your performance impact points, there can be no authenticity in the leadership development process. By the same token, once you select the impact points and how to measure them, you are a long way down the road toward ALD. We hopefully have provided an easy-to-use framework to look at both the nature (typical and extraordinary) of the impact and the level at which the impacts occur (intra- and inter-individual, group, organization, and community). These two dimensions should help you keep in mind the targets you have set.

We think you'll find that most people will take ALD much more seriously if they know where you and they are heading. Indeed, a basic axiom of effective leadership is to know the direction and the goal you have set, and then convey that clearly and in motivational ways to followers. We propose the same is now true for ALD. Hopefully, this chapter has not only convinced you, but also showed you how it can be done.

FOR YOU TO DO IN YOUR ALD JOURNEY

Guess what: We now have a few exercises we want you to do. These will help set you up for the next, final chapter. In Chapter 10 we attempt to tie together and integrate all the material in this book into your own personal ALD plan.

At this point we first want you to think about some positive moments that have occurred either in your life or since picking up this book. Describe how these moments have impacted your thinking about ALD.

Second, we want you to think about any moment that you have created for someone else. Reflect on how you decided to create that moment, how the person responded, and what impact it had on his or her development and performance.

Third, we want you to think about your most enduring work relationships, either in your present position or in previous positions. Now answer the following questions about these relationships:

- How did you first establish your relationship with this person?
- What specific moments or events contributed to the trust you have developed?
- How different are your enduring relationships in terms of how they started and how they then developed over time?
- How diverse are your enduring relationships in terms of the roles these people play in your life and their characteristics, such as gender, age, or experience.
- How have these relationships changed you?
- How have the changes in you changed others around you and their development?
- Name one thing that you have learned from these relationships that has contributed to your performance.

- Can you identify an area in your own performance that you would say is extraordinary? How were you able to accomplish it? What did you learn from that performance achievement, and how are you using that knowledge with others?
- Finally—and this is optional—how many of your enduring relationships would hide you?

We intend to use some of this information as we now move into the last chapter. We want to leave our relationship with you having developed a plan of action with performance impact points for your ALD. Are you ready? (If not, this may be the time to quickly review the whole book or selected chapters or parts again.)

LEADERSHIP NOTES

- *It is important for leaders to establish the distinction between what constitutes typical versus extraordinary performance.* Establishing what constitutes the highest levels of performance can not only facilitate a drive toward excellence, but also establish what may very well become typical or standard performance in the future.
- Leadership impact always starts at the intra-individual level, in that the leader has to help facilitate a change in the way followers think, in order for followers to behave and perform differently. It is important for leaders to keep in mind that change begins in the way each individual views his or her roles, responsibilities, aspirations, and performance impact points. Once that change is in place, making connections between people becomes critically important to sustainable, veritable performance.

■ Great organizations have established a core organizing principle that guides the direction they set, how they work together, and what they ultimately target to accomplish. Too many leaders try to establish multiple core values and principles when one core value can more effectively function as a rallying point for the rest. The idea of having one core value represents the lean thinking concept of "less is more."

10

SOUNDS LIKE A PLAN FOR YOUR ALD

A T THE BEGINNING we stated that our primary goal was to facilitate your authentic leadership development based on what is known from science and practice—in that order. Over the last nine chapters, we have focused on providing you with the various elements that comprise ALD in order to prepare you to build "the plan"—a personal map for your ALD journey so that you can become a "high impact" leader. In our view, the highest impact leaders are those who are the most trusted and who ultimately create veritable, sustained growth and performance. We have no interest in the short-term high impact leaders, who have destroyed some of our most venerable businesses.

As we have indicated throughout, like leadership in general, your ALD must have a plan, a goal, a mission. In addition, as we discussed in the last chapter, you must also have a clear performance impact point in mind in order to successfully execute development and change. In this final chapter, our objective is to help you tie this wealth of material together into something that can be tested by you, supported by you, and ultimately contribute to your ALD.

THE ROLE MOMENTS PLAY IN THE PLAN

The underlying process of ALD, as we have said throughout, frequently begins with some sort of trigger or moment. These "moments that matter" activate an internal review of your core ideas and values, your center, or what we have referred to as your actual self.

These moments trigger something that moves you to think about developing your actual self-concept. This is at the heart of our discussion early in the book about exploring your possible selves. We argued, based on recent work in cognitive psychology, that you don't have one possible self, but many possible selves. Coaching people to explore these alternative selves is fundamental to the ALD process. Without any thought given to your possible selves, there is little basis for ALD.

Trigger moments activate a consideration to move from your current center to a new center of self-awareness and focus, and ultimately leads to action. A fundamental issue for you to consider involves which moments actually trigger in you a sense of such awareness. This should help you initiate a move toward challenging your own view of your authentic leadership potential.

There are trigger moments you can create, and those that life presents according to its own schedule, moments you can then seize to your advantage. In fact, you must seize the opportunities offered by both types of moments in your ALD.

Trigger moments drive enhancements to your self-awareness.
These significant moments that can or do trigger self-awareness can take many different forms. It may be a comment from someone you respect or admire about the need to treat every conversation and interaction you have with those around you as sacred. It may involve someone pointing out that you should focus on what you're good at, and let others work on the areas where you need support. It could be how many positive to negative comments you track each day in your conversations with associates. Or it could be

observing someone who takes the time to make everyone feel as though they are the most important people on earth when they're with him or her.

These moments, whatever form they take, create a heightened self-awareness regarding what you currently do, what you might be able to do, and what you eventually must change in order to enhance your positive influence on others. What follows are several examples of trigger moments that we have observed in our work with ALD.

The Engineer CEO: People vs. Machines

A CEO trained as an engineer was told one day that the work done in his company was actually achieved by people *and* machines, in that order. He had never fully realized that his focus was so thoroughly geared toward how to make machines do things better. To that point, he saw little relevance or value in focusing on people issues. He also struggled to understand why, after optimally designing a technical system it didn't achieve the level of performance that had been planned for it.

Over a period of five years, this engineer went from being a technically oriented specialist, who had been described as one of the least "people persons" in his organization, to one of the company's most revered and respected leaders based on his "caring for people." In the past year, many employees remarked that when this leader came into a room, the trust levels "automatically rose." They all came to believe that he put people first in his calculations of what most contributed to optimal performance.

Taking Off the Brass Knuckles

The president of a financial company was well known for his brass knuckles leadership style for getting the best out of his people. He was tough with everyone around him, and expected them to be tough too, just like him. Then, a few years ago, he realized that though his model of business leadership worked great for wringing efficiencies out of systems, it would not suffice in building an organization that would have unrivaled service quality. For that, a radically different approach would be needed.

This brass-knuckled leader learned that respectful relationships with employees were mirrored in the relationships employees nurtured with their customers. This learning point was a moment that mattered deeply to him. It initiated a complete reevaluation of his leadership style, which continues to evolve today in terms of how he coaches and develops his followers.

The Shy General

A general in the United States Army was extremely shy. It was his nature to be so. Early in his career, he had observed that generals were typically the center of attention at social events, something he felt uncomfortable doing. A close colleague of his told him that he either had to get out of the army business or figure out a way to build the type of climate where people would feel comfortable sharing their ideas and experiences with him.

Afterward, the general reasoned that if he chose someone who had the characteristics people sought in senior military leaders, he could create a climate around himself to increase those types of interactions. So, he decided to bring someone into his senior command team who was at ease interacting in large groups. If this gregarious individual could get people comfortable talking, then, through his association with that individual, the social climate around him would be enhanced. In fact, over time the general noticed that by simply positioning himself close to his talkative associate, the climate around him was more interactive. He also learned some ways to start up conversations built around what he observed from his colleague's successful interactions.

A Manager's Challenged Fix-it Approach

A young IT manager defined being the boss as developing people around him who would then rely upon him for his advice and expertise in correcting their weaknesses. This manager spent most of his time trying to figure out what people did wrong, and then he went about showing them how to fix it. His approach usually resulted in making his people less confident in themselves.

As part of a class ALD exercise, this IT manager was asked to interview someone he always wanted to meet: one of the toughest and most successful college football coaches of all time. He discovered in the interview that the coach's main focus was in positively developing people. Football was secondary to him. In fact, the coach hardly discussed football at all during the interview.

This coach wanted people to leave their interactions with him feeling more capable and confident in themselves. He said he envisioned meeting the young men under his tutelage later in life knowing that he'd helped them discover something important about themselves. They could use this self-awareness to improve how they worked with others.

The coach's long-term vision jarred the young IT manager into a new frame of thinking. After this moment that mattered, he went beyond just having to meet short-term goals on projects, and instead thought about the type of talent in people he needed for projects that had not yet begun. His developmental planning horizon for all of his people was now stretched beyond any point he'd previously considered. This single interview, this moment, caused him to reflect many, many times on whether he was thinking about and developing his followers to their unique potential.

A Sales Executive Adjusts His Style

For most of his career, a successful sales executive in a large financial firm saw every interaction as a potential sale. This sales mentality held whether he was dealing with a product, an idea, or a resource he desired. To his mind, the whole world revolved around transactions and what was in it for him. At the end of the day, he reasoned, how much you sell is what matters to the bottom line, both personally and organizationally.

Some colleagues from other industries, with whom he worked, often spoke about the importance of long-term investments in people. The whole idea of investing in people was anathema to this sales executive, if not to the Wall Street industry in which he worked. However, he respected their views because they were highly successful, and he began to wonder whether investments in people made sense in an industry where people were seen as commodities.

Over time, this star sales exec tried to make slight adjustments in his style. Specifically, he attempted to show more concern for investing in developing the people who worked with and for him. Initially, he encountered a lot of resistance from colleagues in his firm. But over time he noticed that even in the bell-to-bell industry of Wall Street, treating people as individuals with different needs, desires, and expectations not only enhanced his relationships, but had begun to enhance their collective performance.

A Cultural Challenge

A female manager working for a large industrial company was asked to take on an overseas assignment in a country where managers were predominantly male and the cultural values were pronouncedly masculine. She hadn't been involved in any previous overseas assignments, and had significant reservations about her ability to be successful in this proposed assignment.

One evening, a senior leader in the company called her and began the conversation by telling her that he knew she would have reservations about taking the international assignment, which she confirmed. He then discussed with her the need to build respect in different cultures, and pointed out that she had never failed in getting others to respect her for her enormous capabilities—including him. He admitted that he was one of those hard-nosed masculine types, and that she had nevertheless made a huge difference in his own development as a leader. In fact, she hadn't known the impact that she'd had on him until this revealing conversation. He left the discussion saying, "I am sure you can do it again," and she did.

Another Cultural Challenge

A few years ago, shortly after 9/11, Bruce was teaching and doing research in Singapore. One day he sat in on a class in Muslim culture, taught by a Muslim instructor to a group of university (mostly ethnic Chinese) honors students. The instructor spent the first 20 minutes flipping through slides on how the world depicted Muslims; particularly how Hollywood depicted them. He said little about each slide as he flipped through them, one after the other, each showing yet another distasteful stereotypic version of Arabs and Muslims.

Although Bruce travels extensively, he wondered how the average American viewed Muslims, given how they were being bombarded with these images. He realized that these depictions might be their only lens into the Muslim world.

This moment in the Singapore classroom, coupled with the results of a 2001 Gallup Poll that included a large sampling of Muslims from nine countries, profoundly influenced Bruce's thinking on how Muslims are viewed, and how they view us. In the Gallup Poll results, Kuwaiti respondents had the highest percentage (about 40 percent) who thought that the 9/11 attack on the United States was justified. Ironically, of course, it was Kuwait that the U.S. and coalition forces liberated in the first Gulf war with Iraq.

Perhaps these poll results should give all Americans some reason to pause. Why would people we liberated feel such hatred toward us? These moments have stirred in our thinking the need to go much deeper into fully understanding what exactly is causing the feelings about Muslims, and feelings from Muslims, we are now witnessing around the globe. Such moments matter, not only on our perception of the Muslim world, but also to understanding leadership in general in today's global economy.

What we have seen in the above examples is only a small sampling that represents the core focus of this book. That is, there are moments that prompt each of us to look at our center or base. We then must decide whether we need to move from that center to a new position, one where we are challenged to develop to our full potential.

As we noted earlier, these moments can be the result of life's course or can be created and facilitated by situations and circumstances. They can be positive, negative, or simply profoundly interesting. We prefer to not just depend on life's happenings, but to shift and facilitate the focus to the positive.

QUESTIONS TO STIMULATE POSITIVE MOMENTS

To simulate and supplement and/or facilitate life's positive moments, here are some questions to prompt your thinking about some possible starting points for your ALD plan:

- Can you think back to a situation or moment where you learned something that surprised you about some issue related to your own development? What was the nature of that moment? How did it affect your thinking and how you viewed yourself and what you were good at doing as a leader?
- What are you good at in how you go about influencing others? Some leaders are great at communicating an important

message. Some are great at coming up with ideas about the future. Some can bring followers around to their way of thinking, even if it takes a lot of time. Some can get everything organized to move forward. Some just work hard and by example get others to join in and work hard as well. What is your area of optimal performance as a leader right now, whether you are in a formal leadership role or not?

- How could you reinforce that optimal area of capacity in terms of developing one aspect of your leadership that would support it? Do not select one that currently is not your number one capability. What is the closest area of capacity to the one you're good at that can be leveraged to help you sustain optimal performance?

- How would you know you have moved the meter on that secondary area to further support your attaining optimal performance? What is your performance impact point for that supporting area?

- What are some of the steps you have in mind that are needed to achieve the performance impact point?

- What are the real costs and benefits of attaining this performance, because in the beginning the costs, regardless of the benefits, will likely outweigh them?

- What type of support do you feel you need to get to the first step of this impact point, the second step, and so forth? Once you have attained the performance impact point, how can you sustain levels of optimal performance? What type of support will you need to sustain this?

- What is the next area that supports your optimal performance? How can you monitor this area while working on the first one, above, in order to prepare yourself to sustain optimal performance?

These questions can generate specific positive moments, performance impact points, and how to analyze them. However, these are only preliminary to developing your ALD plan.

SOME DEVELOPMENT STRATEGIES

In developing your ALD plan, you need to build efficacy or confidence around what it's possible for you to develop as a leader. The first step is a moment that triggers greater self-awareness. The above questions can help generate such a moment.

The real competition that you will experience is between maintaining your actual self and moving toward some new aspect of your possible self. As we noted previously, there are a number of ways to build your leader efficacy in terms of taking on some new challenge.

You can start by making sure you set yourself up for success, and/or by picking a relevant successful other you can watch to see how they do it. Study what these relevant others do successfully so you can model their behavior. You can also seize moments that would provide opportunities for you to move in a new direction to enhance your actual self. You can ask for someone whom you respect and trust to provide you with the feedback you need to move from your current actual to your new actual by embracing a new possible self.

Regardless of the mechanisms you choose to develop yourself, it will take time and support. You need to stay focused, providing yourself with opportunities to celebrate progress. You need to keep moving toward achieving your new levels of optimal performance.

Remember, you should choose only one area to work on at a time, since it helps you to stay focused. Also, self-development should never occur alone. Make sure you identify people who can support your progress toward achieving the one top priority change you desire.

Referring back to some of the examples that we described in the last chapter on performance impact points, automakers certainly did not go from five years to two years to transform new concepts into actual cars in a year, or even 10 years. It even took Michael Dell a long time to reach his now three-day inventory. Such changes typically occur incrementally over extended periods of time.

In terms of achieving incremental success, ALD is no different. We therefore reiterate the importance of examining ALD in the context of your life program. In this program, you set your direction and milestones by realizing the ALD process can and should continue as you establish new areas to focus on for change.

Perhaps Billy Bob Thornton said it best in the movie *Friday Night Lights*. The locale is the small town of Odessa, Texas, where the high school football team had to win every year and the local townspeople were fanatical about winning the state championship. In their last game at half time, the team is getting their butts whipped by a much stronger team. To paraphrase what the Billy Bob character tells them during that moment: "All year long I have told you to be perfect, and now let me tell you what I meant. We all must come to know what we are each capable of and what is possible. If we achieve the difference between our capabilities and what is possible, then we are perfect, and you can all go out there and be perfect in your own way . . . that's what matters. Be perfect."

Each of us has the ability to achieve our own sense of perfection in our life leadership development program.

You should also realize by now that life's program might not accomplish what you may need to accomplish in terms of authentic leadership development. This is because the right moments may not occur at the right time. So, we are encouraging you to be aware of and choose the moments that will achieve the performance impact point you desire to achieve your own sense of perfection.

You also may be able to take advantage of life's moments for your own development, and then, over time, the development of others.

Drawing from our experiences of working with leaders on their ALD, we are confident that by making you aware of moments that matter, you will be more likely to not only create them, but also take advantage of them as they come your way. This is especially true of the positive moments, not just negative moments such as those many experience during health problems, for instance.

ENGINEERING THE MOMENTS THAT MATTER

If you know your own performance impact point and you know the aspect of the self-concept you want to develop, what comes next is the sequencing of moments that will achieve your optimal performance. In suggesting that you actively arrange moments for your ALD, there are some important points you should consider.

First, you are the author of your own authentic leadership development program. Therefore, selecting the moments is, by and large, your choice. However, they also depend on your sense of self-awareness and timing.

Second, the selection of moments, like life's selection, has its problems. For example, it is not always the right time for a particular moment to have the desired impact on your ALD. Also, not every moment turns out as you might have expected. You have to try—perhaps several times—before the moment actually has the desired impact. It takes a lot of self-awareness and self-regulation to achieve perfection! This also can be just like life.

Finally, while consciously selecting moments and engaging in them, it's likely that moments will come along that you will have to address in life's program. These life's moments may conflict with the goals of your proactive ALD plan. Just like banking your PsyCap, which we discussed in Chapters 7 and 8, you should build in some slack capacity in your ALD plan. This allows you to make adjustments to deal with whatever moments really matter, at the time they matter, to you and others around you.

Specifically, in designing your sequence of moments, there are 10 simple rules to keep in mind that can help guide you, which we present below.

10 RULES THAT CAN HELP GUIDE YOU

1. Choose moments that are as directly related to your performance impact point as possible, and never work on more than one performance impact goal at a time.
2. Most bridges are built to handle three or more times the maximum load required. Follow the same approach, choosing moments that are redundant and can be used like the bridge builders—to structurally reinforce your ALD.
3. Initially, you should overestimate the time it will take to be successful. You can always reallocate extra time if you achieve your goal in less time.
4. Solicit input from others whom you respect and aspire to be like as a leader. The moments that mattered for them may be different, or they may be useful to your development. In either case, getting their input into the moments you have selected could be a positive accelerant for your own development. In so doing, they become part of the moments that matter. You can also engage your peers undergoing ALD. Have them share their moments that matter and impact points, and other positive and negative experiences.
5. Expect nothing dramatic to happen early in the development process. It may all be in your internal self-voice. This is where you experience moments and talk through how they

have impacted your thinking about your ALD. It is likely that you'll impact your thinking way before any behavioral changes or actions occur.

6. As you move from your old actual self to your new one via the awareness of greater possibilities (your possible self), keep in mind that incremental failures, like successes, are often the same. It depends on how you view them in terms of your progress.

7. One of the most natural feelings that will go along with any change and development is some degree of uncertainty. It's natural to feel uncertain during the change process. When we feel completely certain, there is no change happening. You can't possibly move to optimal performance without some degree of uncertainty and without having second thoughts.

8. Assuming a positive scenario, and that you do achieve the performance impact point you set for yourself, keep in mind that "one swallow does not make a summer." In other words, the first time you achieve your performance impact point may not predict a second or a third. However, the main point here is to build some routine around the performance impact point, and some redundancy, until it becomes comfortable, routine, and not associated with uncertainty or doubt. It's here that you think about going from typical to extraordinary.

9. It's always good to keep in mind how you can take advantage of moments that occur by chance in order to help reinforce your new directions. Consider these positive chance moments as a gift you deserve.

10. Based on quantitatively reviewing 100 years of research on leadership interventions and development (see Chapter 3), we have learned that if you believe something will happen, it is more likely to occur. This Pygmalion effect provides

an incredible advantage to achieving your performance impact point. Consequently, if you simply can't fathom the end point for your performance impact goal, then choose an interim point that you believe is achievable. If you can't believe in it, you can't achieve it. So pick the goal that stretches your belief in being successful to the furthest point, but no further.

The basic elements of the ALD plan include a heightened self-awareness around a targeted area where you desire to have a performance impact. The plan needs specific milestones, support systems, resources, and contingencies to adjust to unexpected moments. Thus, the discipline of the plan discussed for ALD is in fact like many other planning processes that you've probably experienced in your career. The main difference here is that you are the target of the plan. With other plans, there is typically an external target.

Your personal ALD plan is more difficult to articulate and execute. It will require that you figure out ways to step back from observing your self-concept. You need to objectively gauge how far along you are in terms of achieving this plan's milestones. Receiving feedback from trusted others will help facilitate your progress toward moving to a new actual self, particularly during the early stages of change.

MAKING THE PLAN WORK

We have learned from our research on leadership and genetics (the born versus made debate) that almost two-thirds of leadership capability can be developed. Each of us typically has considerable reserve capacity for leading. Unfortunately, this potential—unused leadership capacity—lays dormant. Thus, part of developing leadership involves tapping into your latent potential and talent. The key is to find the ways you can influence others that is optimal for you and your leadership challenges.

Almost two-thirds of leadership development is shaped by what happens in life.

An essential point to keep in mind is that there are many different talents that can contribute to successful and effective leadership. You can influence people to pursue a mission in numerous ways. A sampling would include: the ideas you share with them; the commitment you display to them; your willingness to sacrifice and take risks for them; your understanding of their unique needs; the consistency you display between your core belief/value and your actions; your human, social, and psychological capital; and your sense of fairness, integrity, and justice.

There are as many routes to "perfection" as the range of talents you have available to you and your followers. But there are also some basic guidelines to keep in mind if you want to improve your chances of being successful. As we conclude the book, we present a final list, this one of a dozen effective authentic leadership guidelines we can provide you, drawn from both science and actual practice.

A DOZEN LEADERSHIP GUIDELINES

1. Every follower wants to believe that you know who they are, what they desire, and what they want to accomplish. Followers identify with you to the degree that you can build identification with them.

2. You must make sure that every follower fully understands the main message that guides the future direction you have chosen to pursue. They need to be able to articulate that message in their words, not yours, and to make it relevant to their situation.

3. Each follower needs to feel that his or her contribution is greater because they are working together toward a common cause, an agreed upon common goal.

4. People need to be constantly reminded what's important, and what's not.

5. You must be consistent with your principles, beliefs, and values. Otherwise trust will not be established.

6. You need to provide appropriate reinforcing recognition for the contributions made by each follower. It has to be something that would appeal to them, not necessarily to you.

7. Share with your followers things you know and things you want to accomplish in the future.

8. Indicate how you want to engage followers, and then publicly reinforce the way you want followers to engage you and others.

9. Build ownership in the mission you are pursuing. Ownership is not something that is directed or mandated; it is something that becomes part of the individual's self-concept.

10. Build PsyCap (confidence, hope, optimism, and resiliency) in yourself and others by setting up for and reinforcing success rather than problems and failure.

11. Focus on what you do well, and find others to complement areas that are not your areas of strength.

12. Explore the future with others and help each other bring it to the present.

To make your ALD plan work, it also has to be part of the ALD plan of your followers. Because you are the leader, any growth you experience should naturally have an impact on the growth of those around you. As you become more comfortable working through your own plan, you should be able to comfortably share what you have learned with others.

An example of such openness to share would be Fujio Cho, the president of Toyota. He has said the following about being open to everyone about what they have learned over the years: "From the very beginning, Toyota learned much from other carmakers. Sharing what we have discovered since then is one way we can give something back." Sharing your ALD plan and having it become part of your followers' ALD plans is how you can also give something back.

To end the book, on page 245 we have provided a specific template for you to complete before you immerse yourself in the real world of authentic leadership development. Thus, instead of ending with our words, we believe it is appropriate to end with yours. The act of completing this form will bring you closer to execution and will achieve a goal that we set for ourselves, and hopefully that you have bought into: your full engagement in your own authentic leadership development.

In closing, the single question that perhaps remains for most people is whether they can actually develop authentic high impact leadership. We have come to believe that leadership development represents a subtle but still conscious and proactive choice that is wrapped up in how you define yourself. To develop your leadership potential, to make this all work, you have to move from how you have defined yourself to how you want to be defined. Self-awareness means that I know who I am to the degree that any of us can know at any single point in time.

If you can develop a clear definition of who you are, then you can alter that definition and pursue the change needed to make the new definition of yourself accurate, if not perfect. Once you have this new definition in place, you can begin to take greater advantage of creating the moments that matter to your ALD, and to take full advantage of the ones that life throws your way . . . especially the moments that are the most positive!

LEADERSHIP NOTE

Every moment matters to authentic leadership development. This final note is the summary statement for this book.

FINAL CHECKLIST IN YOUR ALD PLAN

Complete this for your new self:

1. Desired impact point: _____

   _____

2. Actual self-definition targeted: _____

   _____

3. Possible self-definition targeted: _____

   _____

4. Core supporting capability: _____

   _____

5. Moment(s) you need to create: _____

   _____

6. Methods to evaluate progress: _____

   _____

7. Milestones: _____

   _____

8. Time to complete: _____

   _____

9. Support required: _____

   _____

10. Secondary capability: _____

    _____

11. Potential obstacles: _____

    _____

12. Next performance target: _____

    _____

Repeat the same cycle for each performance impact point.

FURTHER READING AND RESEARCH SUPPORT

Introduction

Arvey, R. D., and Bouchard, T. J., Jr. "Genetics, Twins, and Organizational Behavior," in L. L. Cummings and B. Staw (eds.), *Research in Organizational Behavior*, 16, 47–82, 1994.

Avolio, B. J. *Full Leadership Development: Building the Vital Forces in Organizations*. Thousand Oaks, CA: Sage, 1999.

Avolio, B. J. *Leadership Development in Balance: Made/Born*. Mahwah, NJ: Lawrence Erlbaum, 2005.

Avolio, B. J., et al., "Unlocking the Mask: A Look at the Process by Which Authentic Leaders Impact Follower Attitudes and Behaviors," *The Leadership Quarterly*, 15 (2004), 801–823.

Bass, B. M. *Leadership and Performance Beyond Expectations*. New York: Free Press, 1985.

Bass, B. M. *Transformational Leadership: Industrial, Military and Educational Impact*. Mahwah, NJ: Lawrence Erlbaum, 1998.

Badaracco, J. L. *Defining Moments: When Managers Must Choose Between Right and Right*. Cambridge, MA: Harvard Business School Press, 1997.

Bennis, W. "The Seven Ages of the Leader," *Harvard Business Review*, January 2004, 1–10.

Clifton, D. O., and Harter, J. K. "Strengths Investment," in K. S. Cameron, J. E. Dutton, and R. E. Quinn (eds.), *Positive Organizational Scholarship*. San Francisco: Berrett-Koehler, 2003.

Conger, J. A. "Developing Leadership Capability: What's Inside the Black Box?" *Academy of Management Executives*, 18 (2004), 136–139.

Fredrickson, B. L. "The Complex Dynamics of Human Flourishing: Toward a General Theory of Positivity," unpublished manuscript, University of Michigan, Ann Arbor, 2004.

Gardner, J. W. *On Leadership.* New York: Free Press, 1993.

Gardner, W. L., et al. "Can You See the Real Me? A Self-Based Model of Authentic Leader and Follower Development," *The Leadership Quarterly* (2005), in press.

George, B. *Authentic Leadership: Rediscovering the Secrets of Creating Lasting Value.* San Francisco: Jossey-Bass, 2003.

Harter, S. "Authenticity," in C. R. Snyder and S. Lopez (eds.), *Handbook of Positive Psychology.* Oxford, UK: Oxford University Press, 2002, 382–394.

Johnson, A. M., et al. "Nature vs. Nurture: Are Leaders Born or Made? A Behavior Genetic Investigation of Leadership Style," *Twin Research,* 1 (1998), 216–223.

Losada, M. "The Complex Dynamics of High Performance Teams," *Mathematical Modeling,* 30 (1999), 179–192.

Luthans, F. "Authentic Leadership: A Positive Developmental Approach," in K. S. Cameron, J. E. Dutton, and R. E. Quinn, *Positive Organizational Scholarship.* San Francisco: Berrett-Koehler, 2003.

Luthans, F., Norman, S., and Hughes, L. "Authentic Leadership: A New Approach for a New Time," in R. Burke and C. Cooper (eds.), *Inspiring Leaders.* London: Routledge, 2005.

May, D. R., et al. "Developing the Moral Component of Authentic Leadership," *Organizational Dynamics,* 32 (2003), 247–260.

Mintzberg, H. *Managers Not MBAs: A Hard Look at the Soft Practice of Managing and Management Development.* San Francisco: Berrett-Koehler, 2004.

Chapter 1

Avolio, B. J., et al. "Unlocking the Mask: A Look at the Process by Which Authentic Leaders Impact Follower Attitudes and Behaviors," *The Leadership Quarterly,* 15 (2004), 801–823.

Bennis, W. G. "The Crucibles of Authentic Leadership," in J. Antonakis, A. T. Gianciolo, and R. J. Sternberg (eds.), *The Nature of Leadership.* Thousand Oaks, CA: Sage, 2003.

Bennis W. G., and Thomas, R. J. *Geeks and Geezers.* Cambridge, MA: Harvard Business School Press, 2002.

Bruner, J. S. *Actual Minds, Possible Selves.* Cambridge, MA: Harvard University Press, 1986.

Campbell, J. D., Chew, B., and Scratchley, L. S. "Cognitive and Emotional Reactions to Daily Events: The Effects of Self-Esteem and Self-Complexity," *Journal of Personality,* 59 (1991), 473–505.

Day, D. V., "Leadership Development: A Review in Context," *The Leadership Quarterly,* 11 (2000), 581-614.

Eden, D., and Leviatan, U. "Implicit Leadership Theory as a Determinant of the Factor Structure Underlying Supervisory Behavioral Scales," *Journal of Applied Psychology,* 60 (1975), 736–741.

Gabriel, Y. *Storytelling in Organizations: Facts, Fictions, and Fantasies.* Oxford, UK: Oxford University Press, 2000.

Harter, S. "Authenticity," in C. R. Snyder and S. J. Lopez (eds.), *Handbook of Positive Psychology.* Oxford, UK: Oxford University Press, 2002.

Kark, R., and Shamir, B. "The Dual Effect of Transformational Leadership: Priming Relational and Collective Selves and Further Effects on Followers," in B. J. Avolio and F. J. Yammarino (eds.), *Transformational and Charismatic Leadership: The Road Ahead,* Vol. 2. Oxford, UK: Elsevier Science, 2002, 67–91.

Kegan, J. *The Evolving Self: Problem and Process in Human Development.* Cambridge, MA: Harvard University Press, 1982.

Lord, R. G., "An Information Processing Approach to Social Perceptions, Leadership, and Behavioral Measurement in Organizations," *Research in Organizational Behavior,* 7 (1985), 87–128.

Lord, R. G., and Brown, D .J. *Leadership Processes and Follower Self-Identity.* Mahwah, NJ: Lawrence Erlbaum, 2004.

Lord, R.G., and Maher, K. J. *Leadership and Information Processing: Linking Perceptions and Performance.* Boston: Unwind Hyman, 1991.

Markus, H., and Nurius, P. "Possible Selves," *American Psychologist,* 41 (1986), 954–969.

Markus, H., and Wurf, E. "The Dynamic Self-Concept: A Psychological Perspective," *Annual Review of Psychology,* 38 (1987), 299–337.

McCall, M. W., Lombardo, M. M., and Morrison, A. M. *The Lessons of Experience.* Lexington, MA: D. C. Heath, 1988.

McCauley, C. D., et al. *Management Development Through Job Experiences: An Annotated Bibliography.* Greensboro, NC: Center for Creative Leadership, 1998.

Morrow, J. E. "Assessing the Developmental Components of Managerial Jobs," *Journal of Applied Psychology,* 79 (1994), 544–560.

Pallus, C. J., Nasby, W., and Easton, R. D. "Understanding Executive Performance: A Life-Story Approach," Report Number 148 (1991), Greensboro, NC: Center for Creative Leadership, 1991.

Roberts, L. M., et al. "Composing the Reflected Best Self-Portrait: Building Pathways for Becoming Extraordinary in Work Organizations," *Academy of Management Review,* in press.

Ruvolo, A. P., and Markus, H. R. "Possible Selves and Performance: The Power of Self-Relevant Imagery," *Social Cognition,* 10 (1992), 95–124.

Silvia, P. J., and Duval, T. S. "Objective Self-Awareness Theory: Recent Progress and Enduring Problems," *Personality and Social Psychology Review,* 5 (2001), 230–241.

Chapter 2

Avolio, B. J. "Examining the Full Range Model of Leadership: Looking Back to Transform Forward," in D. Day and S. Zaccarro (eds.), *Leadership Development for Transforming Organizations.* Mahwah, NJ: Lawrence Erlbaum, 2002.

Bass, B. M., and Avolio, B. J. *Improving Organizational Effectiveness Through Transformational Leadership.* Thousand Oaks, CA: Sage, 1994.

Bono, J., and Judge, T. "Self-Concordance at Work: Toward Understanding the Motivational Effects of Transformational Leadership," *Academy of Management Journal,* 46 (2003), 554–571.

Cameron, K. S., Dutton, J. E., and Quinn, R.E. *Positive Organizational Scholarship.* San Francisco: Berrett-Koehler, 2003.

Conger, J. "Developing Leadership Capability: What's Inside the Black Box?" *Academy of Management Executive,* 18 (2004), 136–139.

Gardner, J. *On Leadership.* New York: Free Press, 1990.

House, R. J., et al. *Culture, Leadership and Organizations: The GLOBE Study of 62 Societies.* Thousand Oaks, CA: Sage, 2004.

Judge, T. A., and Piccolo, R. F. "Transformational and Transactional Leadership: A Meta-Analytic Test of Their Relative Validity," *Journal of Applied Psychology,* 89 (2004), 755–768.

Chapter 3

Arvey, R. D., et al. "The Determinants of Leadership: The Role of Genetic, Personality, and Cognitive Factors," paper presented at the 18th Annual Conference of the Society of Industrial and Organizational Psychology, Orlando, FL, April 11, 2003.

Avolio, B. J. *Full Leadership Development: Building the Vital Forces in Organizations.* Thousand Oaks, CA: Sage, 1999.

Barling, J., Weber, T., and Kelloway, E. K. "Effects of Transformational Leadership Training on Attitudinal and Financial Outcomes," *Journal of Applied Psychology,* 81 (1996), 827–832.

Bass, B. M. *Transformational Leadership: Industrial, Military and Educational Impact.* Mahwah, NJ: Lawrence Erlbaum, 1998.

Bryman, A. S. *Charisma and Leadership in Organizations.* Thousand Oaks, CA: Sage, 1993.

Bryman, A. S. "Charismatic Leadership in Business Organizations," *Leadership Quarterly,* 4 (3/4) (1993), 289–305.

Dvir, T., et al. "Impact of Transformational Leadership Training on Follower Development and Performance: A Field Experiment," *Academy of Management Journal,* 45 (2002), 735–744.

Eden, D., and Sulimani, R. "Pygmalion Training Made Effective: Greater Mastery through Augmentation of Self-Efficacy and Means Efficacy," in B. J. Avolio and F. J. Yammarino (eds.), *Transformational/Charismatic Leadership: The Road Ahead.* Oxford, UK: Elsevier, 2002.

London, M. *Leadership Development: Paths to Self-Insight and Professional Growth.* Mahwah, NJ: Lawrence Erlbaum, 2002.

Luthans, F., and Avolio, B. J. "Authentic Leadership: A Positive Developmental Approach," in K. S. Cameron, J. E. Dutton, and R. E. Quinn, *Positive Organizational Scholarship.* San Francisco: Berrett-Koehler, 2003.

Plomin, R. *Genetics and Experience: The Interplay Between Nature and Nurture.* Thousand Oaks, CA: Sage, 1994.

Zaccaro, S. J., and Klimoski, R. J. *The Nature of Organizational Leadership.* San Francisco: Jossey-Bass, 2001.

Chapter 4

Avolio, B. J., and Kahai, S. "Placing the 'E' in E-Leadership: Minor Tweak or Fundamental Change," in R. Riggio and S. Murphy (eds.), *The Future of Leadership Development.* Mahwah, NJ: Lawrence Erlbaum, 2003.

Bandura, A. "Exercise of Human Agency through Collective Efficacy," *Current Directions in Psychological Science,* 9/3 (2000), 75–78.

Bandura, A. *Self-Efficacy: The Exercise of Control.* New York: Freeman, 1997.

Bandura, A. "Social Cognitive Theory: An Agentic Perspective," *Annual Review of Psychology,* 52 (2001), 1–26.

Chan, K.Y., and Drasgow, R. "Toward a Theory of Individual Differences and Leadership: Understanding the Motive-to-Lead," *Journal of Applied Psychology,* 86 (2001), 481–498.

Choi, Y., and Mai-Dalton, R. R. "On the Leadership Function of Self-Sacrifice," *The Leadership Quarterly,* 9 (1998), 475–501.

Choi, Y., and Mai-Dalton, R. R. "The Model of Followers' Responses to Self-Sacrificial Leadership: An Empirical Test," *The Leadership Quarterly,* 10 (1999), 397–421.

Dvir, T., and Shamir, B. "Follower Developmental Characteristics as Predictors of Predicting Transformational Leadership: A Longitudinal Field Study," *The Leadership Quarterly,* 14 (2003), 327–344.

Eden, D. "Means Efficacy: External Sources of General and Specific Subjective Efficacy," in M. Erez, U. Kleinbeck, and H. Thierry (eds.), *Work Motivation in the Context of a Globalizing Economy.* Mahwah, NJ: Lawrence Erlbaum, 2001, 65–77.

Eden, D., and Zuk, Y. "Seasickness as a Self-Fulfilling Prophecy: Raising Self-Efficacy to Boost Performance at Sea," *Journal of Applied Psychology,* 80 (1995), 628–625.

Howell, J. M., and Shamir, B. "Followers' Role in the Charismatic Leadership Process: Relationships and Their Consequences," *Academy of Management Review,* 30 (2005), 96–112.

Stajkovic, A.D., and Luthans, F. "Self-Efficacy and Work-Related Performance: A Meta-Analysis," *Psychological Bulletin,* 124 (1998), 240–261.

Stajkovic, A.D., and Sommer, S. "Self-Efficacy and Causal Attributions: Direct and Reciprocal Links," *Journal of Applied Social Psychology,* 30 (2000), 707–737.

Staw, B. "Knee Deep in the Big Muddy: A Study of Escalating Commitment to a Chosen Course of Action," *Organizational Behavior and Human Performance,* 16 (1976), 405–433.

Wood, R. E., and Bandura, A. "Impact of Conceptions of Ability on Self-Regulatory Mechanisms and Complex Decision Making," *Journal of Personality and Social Psychology,* 56 (1989), 407–415.

Wood, R. E., and Bandura, A. "Social Cognitive Theory of Organizational Management," *Academy of Management Review,* 14 (1989), 361–384.

Zaheer, A., McEvily, B., and Perrone, V. "Does Trust Matter? Exploring the Effects of Interorganizational and Interpersonal Trust on Performance," *Organization Science,* 9 (1998), 141–159.

Chapter 7

Adler, P. S., and Kwon, S. "Social Capital: Prospects for a New Concept," *Academy of Management Review,* 27 (2002), 17–40.

Bandura, A. "Cultivate Self-Efficacy for Personal and Organizational Effectiveness," in E. A. Locke (ed.), *Handbook of Principles of Organizational Behavior.* Oxford, UK: Blackwell, 2000, 120–136.

Bandura, A. "Exercise of Human Agency through Collective Efficacy," *Current Directions in Psychological Science,* 9 (2000), 75–78.

Bandura, A. "Moral Disengagement in the Perpetuation of Inhumanities," *Personality and Social Psychology Review,* 33 (1999), 193–209.

Bandura, A. "Regulation of Cognitive Processes through Perceived Self-Efficacy," *Developmental Psychology,* 25 (1989), 729–735.

Bandura, A. *Self-Efficacy: The Exercise of Control.* New York: Freeman, 1997.

Bandura, A. "Self-Efficacy Mechanism in Human Agency," *American Psychologist,* 37 (1982), 122–147.

Bandura, A. "Self-Efficacy: Toward a Unifying Theory of Behavioral Change," *Psychological Review,* 84 (1977), 191–215.

Bandura, A. "Social Cognitive Theory: An Agentic Perspective," *Annual Review of Psychology,* 52 (2001), 1–26.

Bandura, A., "Social Cognitive Theory of Self-Regulation," *Organizational Behavior and Human Decision Processes,* 50 (1991), 248–287.

Bandura, A. *Social Foundations of Thought and Action*. Englewood Cliffs, NJ: Prentice-Hall, 1986.

Buckingham, M., and Coffman, C. *First Break All the Rules: What the World's Greatest Managers Do Differently*. New York: Simon and Schuster, 1999.

Cameron, K., Dutton, J., and Quinn, R. (eds.). *Positive Organizational Scholarship*. San Francisco: Berrett-Koehler, 2003.

Coutu, D. L. "How Resilience Works," *Harvard Business Review*, 80/5 (2002), 46–55.

Csikszentmihalyi, M. *Good Business: Leadership, Flow, and the Making of Meaning*. New York: Penguin Books, 2003.

Egeland, B., Carlson, E., and Stroufe, L. A. "Resilience as a Process," *Development and Psychopathology*, 5 (1993), 517–528.

Fredrickson, B. L. "The Role of Positive Emotions in Positive Psychology: The Broaden and Build Theory of Positive Emotions," *American Psychologist*, 56 (2001), 218–226.

Fredrickson, B. L., and Joiner, T. "Positive Emotions Trigger Upward Spirals Toward Emotional Well-Being," *Psychological Science*, 13 (2002), 172–175.

Harter, J., Schmidt, F., and Hayes, T. "Business-Unit-Level Relationship Between Employee Satisfaction, Employee Engagement, and Business Outcomes: A Meta-Analysis," *Journal of Applied Psychology*, 87 (2002), 268–279.

Keyes, C., and Haidt, J. *Flourishing: Positive Psychology and the Life Well-Lived*. Washington, DC: American Psychological Association, 2003.

Kobsa, S. C. "The Hardy Personality," in G. S. Sanders and J. Suls (eds.), *Social Psychology of Health and Illness*. Mahwah, NJ: Lawrence Erlbaum, 1982.

Lepak, D. P., and Sneill, S. A. "The Human Resource Architecture: Toward a Theory of Human Capital Allocation," *Academy of Management Review*, 24 (1999), 31–48.

Lev, B. *Intangibles: Management, Measurement and Reporting*. Washington, DC: Brookings Institution Press, 2001.

Luthans, F. "The Need for and Meaning of Positive Organizational Behavior," *Journal of Organizational Behavior*, 23 (2002), 695–706.

Luthans, F. "Positive Organizational Behavior," *Academy of Management Executive*, 16 (2002), 57–72.

Luthans, F., et al. "Positive Approach to Leadership," *Journal of Leadership Studies*, 8 (2002), 3–20.

Luthans, F., et al. "The Psychological Capital of Chinese Workers: Exploring the Relationship with Performance," *Management and Organization Review*, 1 (2005), 247–269.

Luthans, F., and Avolio, B. J. "Authentic Leadership Development," in K. S. Cameron, J. E. Dutton, and R. E. Quinn (eds.), *Positive Organizational Scholarship*. San Francisco: Berrett-Koehler, 2003, 241–258.

Luthans, F., and Jensen, S. M. Hope: "A New Positive Strength for Human Resource Development," *Human Resource Development Review*, 1 (2002), 304–322.

Luthans, F., Luthans, K. W., and Luthans, B. C. "Positive Psychological Capital: Beyond Human and Social Capital," *Business Horizons*, 47 (2004), 45–50.

Luthans, F., and Peterson, S. J. "Employee Engagement and Manager Self-Efficacy: Implications for Managerial Effectiveness and Development," *Journal of Management Development*, 21 (2002), 376–387.

Luthans, F., and Youssef, C. M. "Human, Social, and Now Positive Psychological Capital Management," *Organizational Dynamics*, 33 (2004),143–160.

Masten, A. S. "Ordinary Magic: Resilience Process in Development," *American Psychologist*, 56 (2001), 227–239.

Masten, A. S., and Reed, M. J. "Resilience in Development," in C. R. Snyder and S. Lopez (eds.), *Handbook of Positive Psychology*. Oxford, UK: Oxford University Press, 2002, 74–88.

Peterson, C., "The Future of Optimism," *American Psychologist*, 55 (2000), 44–55.

Peterson, S., and Luthans, F., "The Positive Impact and Development of Hopeful Leaders," *Leadership and Organization Development Journal*, 24 (2003), 26–31.

Pfeffer, J. *The Human Equation*. Cambridge, MA: Harvard Business School Press, 1998.

Rath, T., and Clifton, D. O. *How Full Is Your Bucket?: Positive Strategies for Work and Life*. New York: Gallup Press, 2004.

Reivich, K., and Shatte, A. *The Resilience Factor: Seven Essential Skills for Overcoming Life's Inevitable Obstacles*. New York: Random House, 2002.

Ryff, C., and Singer, B. "Flourishing Under Fire: Resilience as a Prototype of Challenged Thriving," in C. Keyes, and J. Haidt (eds.), *Flourishing: Positive Psychology and the Life Well-Lived.* Washington, DC: American Psychology Association, 2003, 15–36.

Scheier, M. F., and Carver, C. S. "The Effects of Optimism of Psychological and Physical Well-Being," *Cognitive Theory and Research,* 16 (1992), 201–228.

Schneider, S. L. "In Search of Realistic Optimism," *American Psychologist,* 56 (2001), 250–263.

Seligman, M. *Learned Optimism.* New York: Pocket Books, 1998.

Seligman, M. *Authentic Happiness.* New York: Free Press, 2002.

Seligman, M., and Csikszentmihalyi, M. "Positive Psychology, " *American Psychologist,* 55 (2000), 5–14.

Snyder, C. R. "Conceptualizing, Measuring, and Nurturing Hope," *Journal of Counseling and Development,* 73 (1995), 355–360.

Snyder, C. R. "Managing for High Hope," *R and D Innovator,* 4 (1995), 6–7.

Snyder, C. R. *Handbook of Hope.* San Diego: Academic Press, 2000.

Snyder, C. R., and Lopez, S. *Handbook of Positive Psychology.* Oxford, UK: Oxford University Press, 2002.

Snyder, C. R., et al. "Development and Validation of the State Hope Scale," *Journal of Personality and Social Psychology,* 70 (1996), 321–335.

Snyder, C. R., et al. "The Will and the Ways: Development and Validation of an Individual-Differences Measure of Hope," *Journal of Personality and Social Psychology,* 60 (1991), 570–585.

Snyder, C. R., Rand, K. L., and Sigmon, D. R. "Hope Theory," in C. R. Snyder, and S. Lopez (eds.), *Handbook of Positive Psychology.* Oxford, UK: Oxford University Press, 2002, 257–276.

Sutcliffe, K. M., and Vogus, T. "Organizing for Resilience," in K. S. Cameron, J. E. Dutton, and R. E. Quinn (eds.), *Positive Organizational Scholarship.* San Francisco: Berrett-Koehler, 2003, 94–110.

Chapter 8

Avolio, B. J. *Full Leadership Development: Building the Vital Forces in Organizations.* Thousand Oaks, CA: Sage, 1999.

Avolio, B. J. *Leadership Development in Balance: Made/Born.* Mahwah, NJ: Lawrence Erlbaum, 2005.

Bass, B. M. *Leadership and Performance Beyond Expectations.* New York: Free Press, 1985.

Bass, B. M., and Avolio, B. J. "Transformational Leadership: A Response to Critiques," in M. M. Chemers, and R. Ayman (eds.), *Leadership Theory and Research: Perspectives and Directions.* San Diego: Academic Press, 1993, 49–80.

Bass, B.M., and Steidlmeier, P. "Ethics, Character and Authentic Transformational Leadership," *The Leadership Quarterly,* 10 (1999), 181–217.

Burns, J. M. *Leadership.* New York: Free Press, 1978.

Eden, D. *Pygmalion in Management.* Washington, DC: Heath, 1990.

Gardner, W. L., and Avolio, B. J. "The Charismatic Relationship: A Dramaturgical Perspective," *Academy of Management Review,* 23 (1998), 32–58.

Geyer, A.L.J., and Steyrer, J. M. "Transformational Leadership and Objective Performance in Banks," *Applied Psychology: An International Review,* 47 (1998), 397–420.

Collins, J. *Going from Good to Great: Why Some Companies Make the Leap and Others Don't.* New York: HarperCollins, 2001.

Hater, J. J., and Bass, B. M. "Superiors' Evaluations and Subordinates' Perceptions of Transformational and Transactional Leadership," *Journal of Applied Psychology,* 73 (1988), 695–702.

Howell, J. P. "Two Faces of Charisma: Socialized and Personalized Leadership in Organizations," in J. A. Conger and R. N. Kanungo (eds.), *Charismatic Leadership: The Elusive Factor in Organizational Effectiveness.* San Francisco: Jossey-Bass, 1992.

Kark, R., Shamir, B., and Chen , G. "The Two Faces of Transformational Leadership: Empowerment and Dependency," *Journal of Applied Psychology,* 2 (2003), 246–255.

Lowe, K. B., Kroeck, K. G., and Sivasubramaniam, N. "Effectiveness Correlates of Transformational and Transactional Leadership: A Meta-Analytic Review of the Literature," *The Leadership Quarterly,* 7 (1996), 385–425.

Luthans, F., and Avolio, B. J. "Authentic Leadership: A Positive Developmental Approach," in K. S. Cameron, J. E. Dutton, and R. E. Quinn, *Positive Organizational Scholarship.* San Francisco: Berrett-Koehler, 2003.

Luthans, F., et al. "The Psychological Capital of Chinese Workers: Exploring the Relationship with Performance," *Management and Organization Review,* 1 (2005), 247–269.

Martinko, M. J., and Gardner, W. L. "Learned Helplessness: An Alternative for Performance Deficits," *Academy of Management Review,* 7 (1982), 413–417.

Price, T. "The Ethics of Authentic Transformational Leadership," *The Leadership Quarterly,* 14 (2003), 67–82.

Salovey, P., and Mayer, J. D. "Emotional Intelligence," *Imagination, Cognition, and Personality,* 9 (1990), 185–211.

Youssef, C., and Luthans, F. "Resiliency Development of Organizations, Leaders, and Employees: Multilevel Theory-Building for Sustained Performance," in B. Avolio, W. Gardner, and F. Walumbwa (eds.), *Monographs in Leadership and Management: Authentic Leadership Development,* Oxford, UK: Elsevier.

Chapter 9

Avolio, B. J. "Examining the Full Range Model of Leadership: Looking Back to Transform Forward," in D. Day and S. Zaccarro (eds.), *Leadership Development for Transforming Organizations.* Mahwah, NJ: Lawrence Erlbaum, 2002.

Avolio, B. J. *Leadership in Balance: Made/Born.* Mahwah, NJ: Lawrence Erlbaum, 2005.

Bass, B. M., and Avolio, B. J. *Improving Organizational Effectiveness through Transformational Leadership.* Thousand Oaks, CA: Sage, 1994.

Berson, Y., et al. "The Relationship Between Vision, Strength, Leadership Style, and Context." *The Leadership Quarterly,* 12 (2001), 53–73.

Beng-Chong, and Ployhart , R. E., "Transformational Leadership: Relations to the Five-Factor Model and Team Performance in Typical and Maximum Contexts," *Journal of Applied Psychology,* 89 (2004), 610–621.

Dumdum, U. R., Lowe, K. B., and Avolio, B. J. "A Meta-Analysis of Transformational and Transactional Leadership Correlates of Effectiveness and Satisfaction: An Update and Extension," in B. J. Avolio and F. J. Yammarino (eds.), *Transformational and Charismatic Leadership: The Road Ahead,* Vol. 2. Oxford, UK: Elsevier, 2002, 35–66.

Duvall, S., and Wicklund, R. A. *A Theory of Objective Self-Awareness.* New York: Academic Press, 1972.

Funk, K. "Sustainability and Performance," *MIT Sloan Management Review,* Winter (2003), 65–70.

George, B. *Authentic Leadership: Rediscovering the Secrets of Creating Lasting Value.* San Francisco: Jossey-Bass, 2003.

Hollenbeck, G. P., and Hall, D. T. "Self-Confidence and Leader Performance," *Organizational Dynamics,* 33 (2004), 254–269.

Judge, T. A., and Piccolo, R. F. "Transformational and Transactional Leadership: A Meta-Analytic Test of Their Relative Validity," *Journal of Applied Psychology,* 89 (2004), 755–768.

Lowe, K. B., Kroeck, K. G., and Sivasubramaniam, N. "Effectiveness Correlates of Transformational and Transactional Leadership: A Meta-Analytic Review of the Literature," *The Leadership Quarterly,* 7 (1996), 385–425.

Mayer, R. C., Davis, J. H., and Schoorman, F. D. "An Integrative Model of Organizational Trust," *Academy of Management Review,* 20 (1995), 709–734.

Mumford, M. D., and Connelly, M. S. "Leaders as Creators: Leader Performance and Problem Solving in Ill-Defined Domains," *The Leadership Quarterly,* 2 (1991), 289–316.

Roberts, P.W., and Dowling, G. R. "Corporate Reputation and Sustained Superior Financial Performance," *Strategic Management Journal,* 23 (2002), 1077–1093.

Sparrowe, R. T., et al. "Social Networks and the Performance of Individuals and Groups," *Academy of Management Review,* 44 (2001), 316–325.

Trevino, L. K. "Moral Person and Moral Manager: How Executives Develop a Reputation for Ethical Leadership." *California Management Review,* 42 (2000), 128–142.

Waldman, D. A., et al. "Does Leadership Matter? CEO Leadership Attributes and Profitability Under Conditions of Perceived Environmental Uncertainty," *Academy of Management Journal,* 44 (2001), 134–143.

Chapter 10

Atwater, L. E., et al. "A Longitudinal Study of the Leadership Development Process: Individual Differences Predicting Leader Effectiveness," *Human Relations,* 52, 12 (1999), 1543–1562.

Avolio, B. J., et al. "Transformational Leadership and Organizational Commitment: Mediating Role of Psychological Empowerment and

Moderating Role of Structural Distance," *Journal of Organizational Behavior,* 24 (2004), 1–18.

Conger, J. "Developing Leadership Capability: What's Inside the Black Box?" *Academy of Management Executive,* 18 (2004), 136–139.

Manz, C. C. "Self-Leadership: Toward an Expanded Theory of Self-Influence Processes in Organizations," *Academy of Management Review,* 11 (1986), 585–600.

Plomin, R. *Genetics and Experience: The Interplay Between Nature and Nurture.* Thousand Oaks, CA: Sage, 1994.

Quinn, R. E., Spreitzer, G. M., and Brown, M. V. "Changing Others through Changing Ourselves: The Transformation of Human Systems, *Journal of Management Inquiry,* 9 (2000), 147–164.

INDEX

About the Authors

Bruce J. Avolio, Ph.D., is director of the Gallup Leadership Institute and a Gallup senior scientist. A chaired professor of leadership at the University of Nebraska, Avolio consults with companies around the globe and serves on the editorial boards of several top academic and professional journals. He is the author of *Transformational and Charismatic Leadership* and *Leadership Development in Balance*: *Made/Born.*

Fred Luthans, Ph.D., is a senior scientist with Gallup and a distinguished chaired professor of management at the University of Nebraska. The former president of the National Academy of Management and member of the Academy's Hall of Fame, Luthans has written more than 150 articles and several textbooks, and is the editor or coeditor of a number of academic and professional journals.